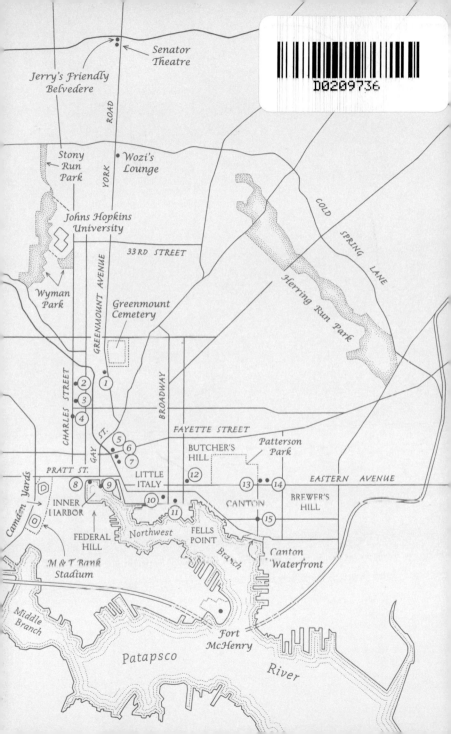

Charm City

TIM CAHILL
Lost in My Own Backyard: A Walk in Yellowstone National Park

ALEX KOTLOWITZ
Never a City So Real: A Walk in Chicago

KINKY FRIEDMAN
The Great Psychedelic Armadillo Picnic: A "Walk" in Austin

MYLA GOLDBERG
Time's Magpie: A Walk Through Prague

ROY BLOUNT, JR.
Feet on the Street: Rambles Around New Orleans

BILL MCKIBBEN
Wandering Home: A Long Walk Across America's Most Hopeful Landscape: Vermont's Champlain Valley and New York's Adirondacks

Charm City

A WALK THROUGH BALTIMORE

MADISON SMARTT BELL

CROWN JOURNEYS

CROWN PUBLISHERS · NEW YORK

Title page photograph © Joseph Sohm; Visions of America/CORBIS

Copyright © 2007 by Madison Smartt Bell

Published in the United States by Crown Journeys, an imprint of the
Crown Publishing Group, a division of Random House, Inc., New York.
www.crownpublishing.com

CROWN JOURNEYS and the Crown Journeys colophon are trademarks of
Random House, Inc.

Grateful acknowledgment is made to the following for permission to reprint
previously published material:

Rooster Blues Records: Excerpt from "Santa's Messin' with the Kids"
by Eddie C. Campbell. Copyright © 1977. Reprinted by permission of
Rooster Blues Records, administered by Jim O'Neil.

G. Schirmer, Inc.: Excerpt from Four Saints in Three Acts, music by
Virgil Thomson, words by Gertrude Stein. Copyright © 1948 (renewed)
by G. Schirmer, Inc. (ASCAP). International copyright secured. All rights
reserved. Reprinted by permission of G. Schirmer, Inc., a subsidiary of
Music Sales Corporation.

Library of Congress Cataloging-in-Publication Data
Bell, Madison Smartt.
  Charm City : a walk through Baltimore / Madison Smartt Bell.— 1st ed.
    p. cm.
  1. Baltimore (Md.)—Description and travel.   2. Baltimore (Md.)—
History.   3. Baltimore (Md.)—Social life and customs.   4. Bell, Madison
Smartt—Travel—Maryland—Baltimore.   5. Walking—Maryland—
Baltimore.   6. Historic sites—Maryland—Baltimore.   7. Historic
buildings—Maryland—Baltimore.   8. Baltimore (Md.)—Buildings,
structures, etc.   I. Title.
  F189.B14B45 2007
  917.52'60444—dc22   2007013208

ISBN 978-0-307-34206-5

Printed in the United States of America

Design by Lauren Dong
Map by Jackie Aher

10 9 8 7 6 5 4 3 2 1

First Edition

For Eric, Glenn, Laura, Jack, and Allison Dickinson
(the invisible walker)—it was a treat to take this trip
with you.

Charm City

Introduction

✎♒♋♦○ ✎♓◆⬡: *A Walk Through Baltimore*—now, what should be plugged into that blank? The city where I live has had a number of nicknames over the years— centuries, that is. A couple of centuries, anyways. My daughter and her friends sometimes call the place "B-more," which might have some value as a functional pun—Be More! Or maybe not.

In the early nineteenth century, some people began to call Baltimore "the Monumental City," for reasons we'll come to in due course. Early in the Civil War, it earned the moniker "Mobtown" (explanation tk; just read on). It's been called "Crabtown" (obvious) and "Nickel Town" (don't ask me why). In the 1980s, it was dubbed "Tiny-town," by the mother of all free alternative listings–based weeklies, the *Baltimore City Paper* (founded 1977); this epithet was a satirical reaction to Baltimore's sudden burst of affectionate self-regard, which took place under the leadership of beloved, diminutive Mayor William Donald Schaefer, a period during which practically all public benches were emblazoned with slogans prominently featuring the phrase "Mayor William Donald Schaefer," which may have struck the early *CP* editors as a bit much. Post-Schaefer mayors really did need to paint something else on all those benches, and so began a fitful effort to rechristen Baltimore "The City that Reads"—a phrase that also adapted itself well to satire: "The City that Breeds," "The City that Bleeds," "The City that Reads . . . at a Third-Grade Level."

Then there's "Charm City," an appellation that has stuck tighter than most, to the point that some people assume and believe that Baltimore was already called "Charm City" back in the days when H. L. Mencken and Edgar Allan Poe walked this patch of earth. Not so. In 1974, Mayor Schaefer commissioned adman Bill Evans to come up with . . . something. Some kind of Baltimore-based gimmick that might appeal to tourists. Evans didn't see much when he first looked around, a few years before the redevelopment of the Inner Harbor put momentum into what became known as a Baltimore Renaissance. "Decaying wharves, rats, and hoboes," Evans reminisced years later. "That was downtown Baltimore. It was pretty bad."

Up came Evans with a scheme wherein tourists on a treasure hunt among Baltimore's then-viable attractions (e.g., Memorial Stadium, home of the Orioles baseball team) would be rewarded at every stop with . . . a charm bracelet. Yeah. Signs went up all over town: "Smile, you're in Baltimore." The charm offensive opened in July 1974, ten days into a garbage collection strike that left mounds of stinking rubbish all over the streets, and which spread to jail guards, sewage workers, a sizable chunk of the Baltimore police force, and also to the keepers of the Baltimore Zoo. Enhanced by a 110-degree heat wave, looting and arson broke out downtown. State troopers were called in. At the zoo, the feeding of smaller animals to the larger carnivores was narrowly averted.

Charming!

But wait. This episode, with all its grotesque irony, alongside the outcome that the zoo animals didn't really eat each other and not too many people really got hurt, turns into a classic *Baltimore thing*. Weird, sometimes disturbingly so, but once you had come out safe on the far side of it, maybe kinda wonderful, too. Only in Baltimore . . . And over the next few years more and more people began to notice that most Baltimore rats didn't have rabies and most Baltimore hoboes wouldn't actually hurt you and that among other choices along the eastern seaboard (at a time when citizens of Boston, New York, or D.C. had to pay a much higher price for a much higher level of urban stress and suffering) Baltimore was an affordable and unexpectedly appealing place to live.

There followed a genuine Baltimore Renaissance, which owed a lot (joking aside) to the leadership of the Schaefer administration.

The bracelets vanished, but *Charm City* hung on . . . because in the end, it's sort of accurate. Baltimore had decided to embrace its peculiarities, in the way that a family learns to cherish the oddities of its more peculiar members. In the later work of John Waters, it becomes more and more obvious that the grotesquerie his films portray is really very amiable at heart. Charming eccentricity (charming on the surface, at least) is the raw material for so many Anne Tyler novels. Beneath the surface there's Poe's dark side with all the horrors it has to offer—but Poe was a *comedy* writer, too, though most people don't remember that. Moreover, Baltimore waitresses of a certain age really do still sometimes call you "Hon."*

Charm City, then. Why not?

---

*This practice was not always limited to women of maternal aspect. Everybody used to do it. Jeff Myers, a Baltimore native now my colleague in the Goucher College English Department, claims to be the last "Hon-Man." In bygone days, he and other Baltimore males had the engrained habit of addressing any and everyone, from lost children to distressed undergraduates to policemen giving them traffic tickets, as "Hon." Once universal and fully gender-free, this locution now strikes people as rather . . . odd, if uttered by a man. Worst case, it might be construed as sexual harassment. Thus the Hon-Man has followed the dodo through the portals of oblivion.

IN THE FALL of 2005, I served as an alternate juror on a trial in the court of the Honorable John Glynn. I'm not going to claim I wanted to be there, but it was a more interesting case than many—a cop-shooting (nonfatal) with enough odd wrinkles that the trial ended with a hung jury. Some aspects of the case struck me as possibly newsworthy, and I got to know the judge a little by asking him questions after the case had concluded. Judge Glynn, who presides over a dispiritingly infinite number of criminal cases, writes a thing or two from time to time—to relieve his feelings, I suppose (a motive he shares with most other writers, including me).

"From the parking lot of The Rotunda, a shopping center near where I live in North Baltimore, I can see the skyline of downtown Baltimore, several miles to the south," Judge Glynn wrote in March 2006. "This is a very small place. If a track traced the boundary of the city, a world-class runner could circle town in less than three hours. Nevertheless, quite a few criminals manage to squeeze themselves within our borders. When one of these criminals happens to be caught, he appears before one of the five judges who try serious felonies in The Circuit Court for Baltimore City. I am one of those judges.

"Each day brings to my courtroom a fresh set of these criminals. . . . The innocent are rarely found outside the nursery, and even more rarely in the Circuit Court for Baltimore City." Examples follow, lots of them. They are weird to the point of being disturbing, and a lot of people don't come out safe on the other side.

Here we have, one might say, a rather *un*charmed view of Baltimore, though it comes from a Baltimore native, born and bred. Judge Glynn is looking at a very small place with a lot of suffering jammed into it. Oddly, most law-abiding citizens of Baltimore don't feel all that much pressure from crime—they don't feel besieged in the way that (to pick one example) law-abiding New Yorkers felt besieged in the 1970s. Many or most of . . . *us* (I guess that's what I'm trying to say here) are as comfortable as people anywhere else in the United States in consuming Baltimore's criminal culture as entertainment on hit shows like *Homicide* and *The Wire* (wonderful, intensely realistic shows which I have enjoyed watching myself). The reason for this oddity, I am reasonably sure, is that the criminals who endlessly stream through courtrooms like Judge Glynn's—they who have made Baltimore number two for murder in major U.S. cities, right behind Detroit—prey almost exclusively on each other. This underclass lives in a parallel universe, cheek by jowl with Charm City . . . yet scarcely touching it, somehow.

There are two cities in Baltimore, then. These promenades try to pass through both of them.

Greenmount Avenue

A T FOUR ON A MID-OCTOBER AFTERNOON, I leave my house and start walking south. I live in Cedarcroft, a neighborhood tucked between two Baltimore arteries—Charles Street and York Road—and just inside the northern city limit. Most people who don't live here never heard of it—a feature I have always appreciated. It was all farmland, back in the day. At the close of the nineteenth century, the city of Baltimore was about an hour's ride from Cedarcroft by buggy or by the horse-drawn trolley cars that served the area since 1842—but, in truth, a world away. The farmers of this area were largely self-sufficient, and visited Baltimore, over the rolled stone roadways of York Road and Charles Street, for major purchases like furniture, farm machinery, and clothing. Today, the land lies just within the Baltimore city limits—just.

Philip E. Lamb bought the first twenty-five acres of the farm he called Cedarcroft in 1885, adding another twenty acres shortly thereafter. The manor house of Cedarcroft Farm still stands a couple of blocks to my east—an enormous, rambling wooden affair with rooms added on rooms like cells of a honeycomb. The drive, which used to unfurl from the big house's portico a quarter mile east to York Road, is now another suburban-style street called Hollen Road. Lamb was a partner, twenty-five years after his first purchase in the area, in the Cedarcroft Land Company, created to subdivide the area. It was an early planned development, supervised by architect Edward L. Palmer.

I live in a two-story stucco house, one of three in an almost identical row, built in the late 1920s, around the same time the sycamores that line these streets were planted, at my best guess. The trees are old now, tall enough to turn each street they shade into something stately, and shedding their leaves early in the drought that has parched the whole region the autumn of 2005.

The neighborhood's changed, the last few years; a generational rollover is well under way. We've seen a lot of old folks die off or move to assisted living, new families with small children moving in. The shady streets are busy with joggers and strollers and dog walkers a good part of each day. There's more small-engine noise hereabout than there used to be, and my neighbor Jack Heyrman, who's been here much longer than I, has a theory that it goes with an influx of Republicans—that leaf blowers, for example, are a strictly Republican appurtenance. Call him paranoid if you will—but Maryland did, not too long ago, elect its first Republican governor since Spiro Agnew.

The leaf-blowing demographic may be watching football now, for somehow it is unusually quiet this pleasant, sunny fall afternoon, with just enough crispness in the air for me to be wearing a light denim jacket. I walk through two quiet blocks of bungalows south of Lake Avenue and turn east in the shadow of the Northern Parkway ramp, where the muffled drone of traffic is almost as soothing as surf. Presently, the street I'm walking on fizzles out, dead-ending at a small derelict park behind a bus stop shelter, which city road workers have fenced off to store their equipment in off hours. I come out into full sunlight, on the corner of Northern Parkway and York Road.

Crossroads. Baltimore is, famously, a checkerboard town, a grid of small contiguous neighborhoods each with its own peculiar character and social constitution. Northwest of this corner is the neighborhood I just walked out of, mostly white, professional, upwardly mobile. Northeast, the other side of York Road, is Chinquapin Park—more modest, more ethnically mixed, with a social dynamic that's maybe more . . . sideways. Every which way. Or call it just impossible to pigeonhole. Southwest is Homeland, a prosperous enclave, notorious for the fastidiousness of its gardens and lawns. Southeast begins a series of lower-income neighborhoods—Govans, Woodbourne, Winston-Govans—with the population getting darker in skin tone the farther south you go.

When I moved to Baltimore in the mid-eighties, I thought it would just be a stop on the way . . . if I thought about it at all. I'd just got married, and my wife was already living in Baltimore, and it seemed a more salubrious place for the two of us than the Brooklyn slum where I was living at the time. Now that we've been here twenty years, I can say that if I had chosen a place to settle instead of just drifting into one, it might have made sense to choose this place. I was born and raised on a farm in Middle Tennessee, and I went to college at Princeton, and moved to New York City for several years after that, and I came away from those experiences with an unconscious wish to live somewhere neither North nor South. Baltimore is a little of both. Some citizens have had a foothold here since John Smith first sailed up the Chesapeake Bay, and some migrated from Poland and Italy and Greece, and a lot of the white folks came from West Virginia, and black folks came from all over the Deep South—both of those last two groups to work in steel, when Baltimore had a steel industry. We're north of the Confederacy here, but south of the Mason–Dixon Line.

Bang across the street is Jerry's Friendly Belvedere, a bar run by a Baltimore Sicilian family since 1978, when Pietro Rugolo bought the place from Jerry Dotterwhite. Dave Rugolo, Pietro's son, has a share in the family's house in the old country and spends a fair amount of time there, which gives him an international perspective, but he's also American to the bone, a sound patriot, and ready to talk politics with you across the bar any day of the week—including Saturdays, generally speaking, though for some reason he's not here today. When I once tried to call him a conservative, Dave pointed out that in fact he backs a good number of liberal causes; at the time, he is the kind of small businessman whom the American right is always claiming to serve and defend, and in fact he seems convinced that that's true.

"My parents came here they had nothing," he's told me. His father had a third-grade education and "never dreamed in ten years he'd own his own business." Pietro Rugolo worked as a mechanic, and Dave's mother worked in a sweatshop, and the family lived in a one-bedroom apartment until Dave was five years old (speaking Italian in the household, so that Dave is still fluent in that tongue). "When I came here the streets were paved with stone," Pietro Rugolo told his sons (Dave's brother, Nathanial, runs another bar called the Crease in Towson). "Now they're paved with silver. For your generation, it should be gold."

"You make that happen," Dave says now. He's got a decent amount of direct experience with class and economic stratification in other countries. "The beautiful thing about America," he says, "is that no one tells you you can't."

Dave is a hardworking guy, I have seen, so I hope maybe he is getting a weekend off. Jerry's is catching a lull at this time of day on a weekend. Daytime and early evening it pulls a mostly blue-collar crowd—people come for the games on the TVs at either end of the long bar, or to eat when the time is right. There's a sit-down restaurant through the saloon doors in back of the bar, oysters in season and once in a while pit beef. Nothing too fancy, but the menu is concocted by the people who actually operate the place, instead of standardized at some corporate headquarters a couple of thousand miles away. Shellfish here is especially good; a guy named Francis brings it straight up the bay. In football season, there's a bull roast every Monday night, with two bushels of oysters and forty or fifty pounds of beef, which Dave and Pietro cook themselves, letting their kitchen staff go for the evening to protect the secret family recipe. By half time, the beef is always gone.

Late nights, sometimes, the demo changes, and the place packs out with the college crowd, from Loyola and Notre Dame a little ways south, or maybe from Towson University farther up York Road. There are games for those customers down in the basement, but Jerry's never gets completely overrun by the college kids, "by design," as Dave puts it. There's long months of the year when the college crowd isn't even in town. "My bread and butter is my regulars," Dave says. "They're family, after you've been here so long."

I'm not that much of a sports fan really (well, maybe during football play-offs), but Jerry's offers another show. If you sit in the L of the bar, you're looking across the counter into the liquor store component of the business, which is small but serious (and open on Sundays). It's hopping this afternoon, of course, since everybody has to stock up for Saturday night, and the clientele comes in all colors, shapes, and sizes. It is an excellent people parade, but I only watch it for the length of one beer, since I have still got quite a long ways to go.

Outside, there's a swirl of traffic from Belvedere Square, a covered market with half a dozen high-end food stalls, anchored by a fancy Italian butcher and a spiffy new wine bar. The whole place went mysteriously vacant in the mid-1990s, until a Buddhist monk I knew as a tai chi instructor did a semisecret ceremony to propitiate the local deities—I know it sounds odd, but whatever it was it seems to have taken the curse off the place, and now Belvedere Square is booming again. Up the hill, the Senator Theatre is playing *In Her Shoes* (which features, among other delicacies, a dizzy blond Cameron Diaz reading a poem by Elizabeth Bishop). The Senator's a gorgeous Art Deco building, with a lovely Palladian dome for its lobby, and the owners have staunchly kept it sailing as a single-screen theater, through waves of home video and multiplex construction, showing a mix of commercial pictures and art-house specials. It's a favorite venue to premiere movies with any local connections—for over a decade, most films by John Waters and Barry Levinson have opened with big festivities here, each commemorated with a flagstone of concrete out front, impressed with the key info and signatures in the style of the Hollywood Walk of Fame. There've been enough of these, I notice, that they are fixing to run out of room.

Soon after Barry Levinson's *Diner* opened in Baltimore, a Pullman diner car materialized on a grassy vacant lot on the high berm across the street from the Senator. Some people said it was the diner from the movie, and some people said it wasn't. Most people expected that somebody would someday do something with it, but nobody ever did. It sat there, settling into its footprint, imperceptibly yielding to the forces of entropy until someone decided to reduce its capacity as an attractive nuisance by surrounding it with a chain-link fence . . . and then, one day, it was gone.

A bit wistfully, I pass, on the next block, the storefront where Master Lee's tae kwon do school used to be. I finally earned my black belt there around 1990, after twenty years or so of intermittent study. I am more persevering than talented as a martial-arts student, it appears. Another student there was an elderly black man named Hunter, who I believed possessed the Rosicrucian secret to the perfect gumbo, which I had eaten once, when I was about nine years old, in a little backwater restaurant on the Mississippi Gulf coast called Mary's Kitchen, where the gumbo was thick black—the color and consistency of roofing tar, but possibly the best thing I have ever eaten, certainly the best gumbo I have ever eaten, and ever since I had been in slow but passionate pursuit of the right way to make a gumbo black and flavorful like that, and I had absorbed a lot of esoterica about okra, filé powder, and how to make a roux; I had made and consumed some very good gumbos, but the ultimate Heart of Gumbo Darkness seemed always to slip beyond my grasp. Well, one afternoon as we were changing after practice, Hunter happened to mention that a lot of his family were coming from Louisiana to visit him for Thanksgiving, which was just a few days away . . . and that he was planning to make a big gumbo for them all. I asked him questions, and he was forthcoming—he didn't seem to withhold anything about his gumbo strategy, yet most of his moves were already known to me, except . . .

". . . and then, I put in the *obeah seasoning* . . . ," Hunter explained.

My eyes lit up. My heart leaped. I had never before heard of *obeah seasoning*. Surely, the Gumbo Grail was almost in my hand. Tell me, Hunter, I implored, what exactly goes into that *obeah seasoning*.

Hunter gave me a funny look. "It's just obeah seasoning."

Okay, it wasn't going to come that easy. "Yes, but what goes *in* the *obeah seasoning*?"

Hunter looked at me like I was crazy. "It's just regular *obeah seasoning*."

We took this around a couple more times until we both became discontented and frustrated, then finally I was made to understand (now, Hunter's Louisiana accent was perhaps no thicker than my Tennessee, but it was different anyway) that what he was saying was *Old Bay Seasoning,* a substance more common in Baltimore than salt. Well, never mind . . .

Toward the top of the rise from the Senator is Govans Presbyterian Church, a gray stone pile, and venerable, locked down for Saturday night. The orange afternoon sunlight comes slanting through the pale old stones that have been settling in the wide graveyard behind the church for more than a century, some of them. The church itself has been standing there since 1844, and many grave markers go back to the mid-nineteenth century. Govans itself has been there much longer; it was at first a crossroads settlement when York Road was an Indian trail, and takes its name from William Govane, a Scot who acquired the tract of land from Frederick Calvert, Lord Baltimore, in the middle of the eighteenth century.

York Road became a turnpike for carriage of produce and goods back and forth from the Port of Baltimore (which is more or less where I'm headed now) and the farms like Lamb's estate that rolled off to the north, back in those days, all the way into Pennsylvania. Finally, in 1818, the expansion of Baltimore City gobbled up old Govanstowne, and within a few years the pace of the development had turned the old turnpike into what was then called a "gasoline alley," a description that still works pretty well today. North of where I'm standing, York Road is one long strip of service stations, convenience stores, fast-food restaurants, car dealerships, and big-box stores that goes all the way to York, Pennsylvania—a vivid example of the scariest urban sprawl. Sprawl has more or less swallowed up a place called Towson, which when I first came to Baltimore still had a few time-warp bars and restaurants that had changed practically not at all since Towson was an autonomous small town, but these have finally adapted themselves to serve the rapidly growing student populations of Towson University, to the south and west, and Goucher College (where I teach) just to the north. For a sense of the old Towson, you can still go look at the beautiful old courthouse, built in the 1850s, or the WPA-style murals in the post office just across Pennsylvania Avenue. The first cabin that William Towson built alongside the Indian trail in 1850 is, of course, long gone.

That old trail ran south through the spot where I'm standing right now. Across the street from Govans Presbyterian there are still a couple of vestiges of an independent Govans village center: Maenner's Market, a vegetable stand that survived as a family business till just a couple of years ago, and Field's Old Trail, another classic neighborhood bar that's been holding its own on this corner since 1934. The afternoon light falls on that corner with a certain kindliness, though the contrast is stark; it is the sort of light that Edward Hopper liked to paint. The car wash a couple of doors farther down is bathed in it, and the glow picks out a muscular, shaven-headed black man, clad in what I'd describe as dress over-alls, putting the finishing touches on his huge, glossy SUV, while his lady friend, high in the passenger seat, studies his work. Behind them, a freehand mural on the brick wall describes the evolution of York Road from the covered wagon, through the trolley cars that long ago rolled along this street, and finally to . . . the municipal bus.

I keep walking, passing the almost unnoticeable Acme T.V. Stereo Service, an old-school establishment where George, the proprietor, will solder up electric gui-tar cords for me on a walk-in and refuse to take my money, which is not the sort of event that happens very much around here these days. At the corner of Wood-bourne Avenue (where the turnpike tollgate used to be in the days of Philip Lamb), a rusty red car comes bomb-ing through a red light—I'm just barely alert enough to skip backward out of its path. Taking an extra forty-five seconds or so on a traffic signal is a fine old Baltimore tra-dition, only slightly eroded by the automatic cameras recently installed at many key intersections—viciously loathed by a great many drivers, taxi drivers especially. Since a consciousness of this light-running habit has been absorbed into the reflexes of most local motorists, there are far less accidents than you would expect.

On the sidewalk beneath the bloodred awnings of the Antioch Ever-increasing Faith International Church, a suite of maroon upholstered furniture is out on the sidewalk, with a handful of young black people lounging on it as if to demonstrate its comfort. One of them has a pair of drumsticks, and he plays a quick solo on a parking meter, putting a responsive bounce in my step as I pass them. I take a glance across the street, at the cheerfully painted Caribbean Variety Store, next to Valik's Liquors, Package Store and Bar, next to the Looking Better Beauty Salon and the China Star Carryout, and then I go back to watching where I'm going. The wind has picked up, swirling brown leaves over the sidewalk. An Asian girl is trying to sweep leaves in front of the Bangkok Restaurant; trim in black trousers and a white blouse, she glances at me shyly as I pass.

To the left, there's the IHOP where I used to take my daughter for pigs in blankets, when she was the size to eat pigs in blankets; its blue shingle roof has been repainted a lurid green, and the building repurposed as an Enterprise Rent-a-Car. Another big gray stone church crops up to my right: Govans Boundary United Methodist. A big black-and-white sign on the portico admonishes NO LOITERING WORSHIP AT 9:30 AM. A little way south, just above Cold Spring Lane, there's a string of little brick row houses, one advertising "Mrs Terrell's Little Angels— Licensed Provider," and another has its stamp-sized yard already done up for Halloween (which will soon be upon us): a handful of cardboard tombstones Magic Markered with R.I.P. FREDDY! R.I.P. JASON! And so on, through the roster of horror-show villains.

At the corner of Cold Spring, I have another near miss with another Bondo-spackled beater, out to prove that red cars have more accidents, if any more evidence were needed. The driver is white—I can tell from the yellow-haired elbow hanging out of the window, and that is as much as I see of him before he has squealed away. I pause for a moment, recalling that some friends of mine once took a stray nine-millimeter round through their vehicle on this selfsame corner—no one injured (Providence be thanked), though the van was full of small children at the time. Driving this corridor is an interesting experience, even without cross-fire incidents, thanks to the jaywalkers who always seem to be aiming straight for the front bumper of your car, their arms and legs robotically stiff and their gaze fixed on some faraway horizon, like zombies from a George Romero movie.

I jaywalk myself, because I am thirsty, timing my crossing so that the oncoming car will just clear my hip, like a bull turning through the matador's cape. From the point of view of the pedestrian, it is a perfectly safe maneuver. Lots of other people are doing it, too. On the east side of the street, I'm suddenly dazzled by the sunlight, and refreshment is not so obvious as I expected. A lot of the people swirling around on the corner are eating early, stand-up suppers, fried chicken or fried fish out of little cardboard baskets, bought from one of the small corner food stands that specialize in "Lake Trout" and the like, and somehow have held their own against the fast-food chains. But Towers Lounge and Package Goods is closed, perhaps forever, from the look of things. New Rex Liquors is open and doing a land-office trade, but it doesn't seem to have a back room. The Gaimei Nangba Nanlon Woah-Tee Multipurpose Neighborhood Center (Courtesy of Bong County, Liberia/MD USA) has a gorgeous mural, featuring pirogues in some fantastic lagoon, painted over the clapboards and around the fili-greed iron of the gates securing door and window . . . but the center isn't open, either, and probably wouldn't have what I'm after if it was.

The amber sunset light is glorious—a light that finds beauty in everything it touches. I'm on the wrong side of the street, however—I have become part of that Hop-peresque view, when I would rather be appreciating it. The sun is low, and shining in my eyes. I trudge past the Agape Christian Church, a storefront much like the restaurants and shops along this stretch of road. Oasis appears a couple doors south in the form of Wozi's Lounge.

Inside the front door is kind of an airlock, a space about the size of an elevator, hemmed in by thick Plexi-glas, blacked out by stickers and hand-lettered posters, the few clear areas opaque from scratches. I've tripped a bell coming in, and presently a shadow appears at the cash register on the other side of the Plexiglas hatch through which I could buy a six-pack or a short dog, were that my mission, but instead I jerk my thumb at the inner door. For sure, I'm not their usual customer, but I must not look too much like an armed robber, either, because after forty seconds of scrutiny, the shadow punches the buzzer and lets me in.

It's barely five; I'm the first one here. It's a short, narrow barroom, almost too dark to see, and reeks of the disinfectant the bartender, a solid black woman with straightened hair, is wiping down the counter with. Over her shoulder is a TV wedged high in the corner: Minister Farrakhan, somewhere in D.C., haranguing what seems to be a "Million More" march.

"As long as we keep our mouth in the kitchen of our enemy, we will never have good health." Farrakhan is running through what I take to be his most recent black separatist platform. The bartender pops open a bottle of Bud for me. At the back end of the bar, the bearded black guy who let me in is drinking a can of Colt 45 Malt Liquor and smoking an extra-long cigarette and talking in a sweet island accent I can't quite decipher. I'm wondering who Wozi is and if she might be a Haitian— switching out *R* for *W* is a standard Kreyol thing to do.

Farrakhan looks a little heavy in his two-toned blue-striped suit, and maybe a little weary, too, but he is still a commanding speaker. His nation needs a Ministry of Agriculture (to get its mouth out of the kitchen of the enemy), and a Ministry of Education, and a Ministry of Arts and Culture, and a Ministry of Defense. "Our young people are fighting in the wrong war," he says, drawing a ripple of applause. "Either against each other at home or in an unjust war in Iraq and Afghanistan." The camera pans over a few ranks of the audience— mostly middle-aged black women in this particular cut-away, wearing their church hats. "You don't need to be in Iraq and Afghanistan," says Farrakhan. "You need to be in our neighborhoods stopping the police from shooting us down."

The rhetoric seems a little tired, and the audience none too thrilled by it. The religious component is dis-tinctly more ecumenical than it used to be in the heyday of the Nation of Islam. Farrakhan has been trying to set up a bigger tent since the first Million Man March ten years ago. The world has not changed tremendously for the better during that time. When he starts talking about "my TV" the barmaid snorts, "Yeah, right." There will be examples of the wrong war on the street outside, once the sun goes down, and probably not so many examples of positive spiritual fellowship. Farrakhan is explaining how to go about giving him money through his website. I drain my beer and get moving.

The sun has dropped behind the buildings on the west side of the street, but the heavy stone gateway into Guil-ford is suffused in a lurid red glow. A black car hovers under the archway, throbbing a mega-bass hip-hop beat; its tires let out the classic squeal as it lurches out into the northbound lane. York Road has changed its name to Greenmount Avenue. Guilford is the most opulent neighborhood on the north side of Baltimore, with parklike, winding streets and magnificent, expensive houses, laid out between 1903 and 1911 by Frederick Law Olmsted and his two sons, whose influence on urban planning all over Baltimore turns out to have been very extensive. Olmsted believed in a "law of progress" in the service of the "cleanliness and purity of domestic life." Cleansing and purifying turned out to involve the formal exclusion of Jews, Catholics, blacks, Italians, and so on, until the exclusionary covenants were struck down by the Supreme Court in 1948. The senior Olmsted was extremely wary of "the unmistakable signs of the advance guard of squalor," by which I think he may have meant what's on the other side of Greenmount Avenue from Guilford, in the area where I am now strolling. "What grounds of confidence can I have," he wondered, "that I shall not by-and-by find a dram-shop on my right, or a beer-garden on my left, or a factory chimney or a warehouse cutting off the view . . . ?" Well, to Guilford's west are some more upmarket neighborhoods, like Tuscany-Canterbury and Roland Park (another Olmsted project), but Greenmount Avenue is more like a frontier, between the haves and the . . . have-lesses, anyway. East of Greenmount, Wilson Park and Pen Lucy and Waverly are far less well-to-do, and enough opportunistic crime leaks through the barrier to keep Guilford in a state of yellow alert.

It's gonna get dark, and the wind is rising. On the next corner, a pair of pale crosses stand out starkly from the black double doors of the Mercy Seat C.O.G.I.C. The string of improvisational small businesses peters out here: Devota's Beauty Salon is closed, and Wild Bill's, the last Lake Trout purveyor on this strip, is locked down for the evening. The houses south are up on a berm, and sheltered by thick foliage right up to the retaining wall, including a couple of lovely weeping willows. A white guy with long gray hair and beard hails me cheerily from the other side of the street: "Jim!" I apologize for not being Jim, walk on.

There's a lull in traffic as daylight fades. I've come two miles in about an hour, not especially pushing my pace. A lone Arab wagon comes rattling up the street; the brown pony in the shafts, with a shaggy blond mane and tail, is punching out an unusually brisk trot for one of these vendors. Baltimore's Arabs (pronounced *Ay-rab*)—or A-rabbers, as they are as often called—have nothing to do with the Middle East. They've been operating so long under that title that nobody knows for certain where they or their name came from. One story has it that their trade goes back to the post–Civil War time when black merchants were excluded from Baltimore's numerous covered markets—so they took to mobile vending instead.

Holler, holler, holler, till my throat get sore.
If it wasn't for the pretty girls, I wouldn't have to holler no
more.
I say, Watermelon! Watermelon!
Got em red to the rind, lady.

The cart is gaily painted, red and yellow—it has a
roof for shelter, but otherwise it's open to display the
produce, although there is no produce now. I reckon
maybe they must have sold out. Sometimes animal lovers
get agitated about the condition of the Arabbers' ponies,
but this one at least looks healthy and strong. The Arabbers are almost all black men, and their surviving stables
are all downtown—thus under increasing urban pressure.
But preservationists have helped keep them going—not
only because of the quaintness of the spectacle, but
because the Arabbers still do certain things that otherwise
wouldn't get done at all. For one thing, they deliver
groceries to shut-ins and the elderly. "We providing a
service for a lot of people who can't always get to the
store themselves," says Earl Dorsey (on the Arabber
Preservation Society Home Page). "We bring it to them.
A lot of people who buy what I've got depend on me."
And the culture offers profitable self-employment for
people who might otherwise be swelling the ranks of the
homeless poor. "It's honest work by people who want
to work hard and maybe have a little fun doing it," says
one, and another remembers, "Fatback used his a-rabbing

profits to put a 'slew' of his sixteen children through college."

The empty wagon rattles past, the pony holding his head high, under the bright metal trappings of his harness. An extra Arab reclines in the back, between the produce shelves, one leg trailing over the tailgate. I turn into York Court number 3, to pick up Eric Singer. The York Courts would be standard Baltimore row houses if not for their setback from the road—the several dwellings share a rectangle of slightly disheveled garden. Technically, these houses are in Guilford, I believe, but the ambience is more that of Waverly, on the opposite side of Greenmount. There's no light on in Eric's place, but after a little bashing on the door he opens it, blinking like a sleepy bear. The long room behind him is a half-cataloged museum of South Africa, whence Eric hails. He has been receiving artifacts from his father, an anthropologist at the University of Chicago.

We keep heading south on Greenmount, dodging overgrown shrubbery that encroaches on the narrow sidewalk, till we hit another commercial strip just north of Thirty-third Street. There's a rich smell of *obeah seasoning* fuming out of the Waverly Crab House—a great place from which to carry crabs home. Crab scarcity, though, has been one of the more depressing pieces of news to come out of the Chesapeake Bay of late, and the price is up to $25 a dozen. Across Greenmount, the Stadium Lounge is open for business still, though its location has been, shall we say, anomalous since Memorial Stadium closed its gates for good in the early 1990s, yielding its place to the new baseball coliseum at Camden Yards downtown. Inside, you can get a mixed drink for a mere $2. There are photos of Cal Ripken, and the whole 1979 Orioles team, and fruit machines on the opposite wall, and the bar mirrors are covered with huge decals for the Ravens football team. Outside, the north wall has been freshly repainted in Oriole Orange, with the baseball team's logo peeping through one circle and natty Mr. Boh, the mascot of National Bohemian beer, through another. When Memorial Stadium was in its prime, the beer and the baseball were yoked together for everybody who went there.

Home to the Orioles from 1954 to 1991, Memorial Stadium also housed the Baltimore Colts for many years. Baltimore loves its pro teams to distraction, and the name of Bob Irsay, the owner who smuggled the Colts to Indianapolis, is still reviled in back rooms all over town. Once the Orioles left, Memorial Stadium stood empty for a decade. Though it hosted the Baltimore Ravens briefly, the football team soon got its own state-of-the-art facility downtown, a stone's throw away from Camden Yards, and though several alternative uses for Memorial Stadium were proposed, none stuck. The building was torn down in 2000, except for the World War II memorial wall facing Thirty-third Street and dominating the entrance, which was finally demolished in 2001. Chuck Yealdhall, who spent about a thousand hours cutting the memorial lettering out of sheets of steel, said, "Maybe people will appreciate it more after they tear it down." Well, maybe . . . Most recently, the site has been refashioned into the Stadium Place retirement community, with an attractive layout and an unusual amount of green space.

I am accounted a fast walker, but Eric, when he puts his head down, is faster still. We step out briskly through the gloaming. A waxing moon is rising to our east over Thirty-third Street. The harvest moon, fat and low to the horizon. In that direction, Waverly keeps going. To our west is Abell Street and the backside of Charles Village, the academic ghetto that fronts on the Johns Hopkins University Homewood campus, west of Charles Street. On these blocks of Greenmount, the cut-rate stores and thrift shops that serve the permanently poor blend into trendier secondhand and vintage stores for temporarily impoverished students and junior faculty. There's a huge farmers' market here Saturday mornings, in a big parking lot south of University Parkway, where you can find anything from smoked pig tails to Somali pastries. On the corner of Thirty-fourth is Pete's Grille, a breakfast and lunch counter that's been slinging some pretty good hash since 1930. West on Thirty-third Street is Normal's, the best buy-sell-or-trade emporium for used books and CDs on the north side of Baltimore. Across the street, Red's Records has been shut down since Red moved its vast acreage of used vinyl to some other town—the space now occupied exclusively, though infrequently, by the local chapter of the Communist Party.

At the crest of the little hill on Thirtieth Street, next to a display window that exhorts us to "Elect Jesus Christ Head of Your Life Forever," we've got a panoramic view all the way to the high-rises of downtown. Between here and there is a wide expanse of urban wasteland. On a southeast corner away down the hill, Saint Ann's church pokes its lonely little brown spire into the darkening sky. Saint Ann's came into being in 1873 to serve a growing Irish population, including one Captain Kennedy, who vowed to found the church if his ship should survive a certain storm, which it did, and its anchor stands in front of the church today.

We start down the grade. A good half of the brick row houses we pass are boarded up with warping plywood. What's open for business are improvisational convenience and liquor stores and fried-fish restaurants, a couple of storefront churches, Heavenly Rest, among others, not far from Out the Gate Bail Bond. What appeals to me really is the Déja Vu, with a small black-and-white emblem of a martini glass on a small square sign hanging over the street, but it's not clear to me that it's open. At Twenty-seventh Street, across from King Solomon's Blue Lodge (a repair of Freemasons, to judge from the emblem), is a vast mural on a several-story expanse of blank brick: "LONG LIVE THE ROSE

THAT GREW FROM CONCRETE" bursts from an aureole of golden light, while under its glow black kids are opening hydrants or playing basketball or poring over a book on a painted sidewalk that only looks a little neater than the real one.

Just above Twenty-sixth Street, a stretch of seldom-used railroad track runs under Greenmount. The storm fence that closes off the cut from the street is heavily overgrown with clematis and honeysuckle vine, and on the east side, white letters wedged into the vine spell out the name of the local community group—HARWOOD 26-ERS. I glance to the west, where this track terminates at the old Mount Royal Station of the long defunct B&O line, and then to the east, where the railroad leaves town along the north edge of the Baltimore City Cemetery.

Eric, meanwhile, is telling me that these were mostly white working-class neighborhoods around here, before the big waves of black migration from the South. Nowadays, the area puts him in mind of the poorer parts of South Africa. It strikes him as ironic now that his parents left to get away from apartheid and ended up in an airtight white enclave in the midst of massively black Chicago. As for Eric himself, he lives with the glories of Guilford at his back, but facing distinctly less-glorious Waverly. By a strict measure, Wild Bill's is the closest restaurant to his house, and Wozi's Lounge the closest tavern—I don't know how much he frequents them, however. Eric teaches politics and runs the International

Studies program at Goucher College, ten miles to the north up this very same street, where I've taught creative writing since the mid-1980s. He has seen a fair amount of the world. Sometimes he sends his students on bus rides through these regions, for a preliminary glimpse of a world that most of them have never seen.

"It wouldn't be a good idea to send them on foot," I suggest.

At that moment, Eric's attention sharpens to a point on a vacant lot south of Twenty-fifth Street, where several people are crouching—making a plan, making a deal? It's unclear exactly what, but Eric makes one of the young women as a recent Goucher alum, known to have been involved in grassroots organization work since her graduation. She seems at least as much at home down here as we do, probably more so, and very much involved in whatever she's doing.

So, without interrupting her by more than a glance, we walk on. Briskly. The twilight is thickening. Plenty of people are milling around on the street. A young man in dreads, wheeling a bicycle, gives us a shout. We return the greeting and pass on without breaking stride. Être Humain is emblazoned in red letters across the back of my denim jacket, the French for "human being," or, if you prefer, "to be human." I am considering the phrase as a tattoo but thought I would try it on a jacket first, and I thought it might be lucky to wear it on this promenade. There is a collapsible police baton in the inside pocket of the jacket and a swing-blade knife clipped inside my trouser pocket, although I don't really think I will be needing either of these implements. It wouldn't have been a good idea to take this walk the day the Simi Valley jury acquitted the cops who beat up Rodney King, or during the nastier phases of the O. J. Simpson trial, but on an ordinary day there's no aggravated racial tension in Baltimore. On the other hand, the most likely reason for a couple of white boys to be walking these blocks on a Saturday night would be to buy drugs. The next best explanation would be that we are undercover narcotics police—"knockers," as they are locally known to some. People sometimes do get into trouble on the basis of such small misunderstandings.

A few months after this excursion with Eric, I will catch a ride to the airport with a car-service driver by the name of John O'Brien. In the forties, when he was a kid, he lived in this area where Eric and I are walking now, on the 2200 and then the 2300 block of Greenmount Avenue. Much of the neighborhood was Irish then and most of it was Catholic, and community life revolved around Saint Ann's church and the school attached to it. In 1956, when O'Brien was fifteen, he moved ten or so blocks up Greenmount to Waverly, to an apartment above a music store, and over the next few years the white working-class denizens of lower Greenmount began to migrate on a northeast diagonal, first to nearby Northwood, and from there to Parkville, and then on to Perry Hall.

He's pretty startled to hear of my walk down that stretch of Greenmount in 2005 . . . though he has been around and not too much surprises him. He was around when both Jews and Catholics were prevented by covenant from buying property in Guilford, and he was around in the days when a sign on the gate of a swimming pool in Mount Washington read NO DOGS OR JEWS ALLOWED. In his prime, O'Brien was an ace thrift shopper, and could deck himself out in Armani for special nights on the town—nobody could tell or needed to know that he was working in a tire factory down in lower Hampden. One night, he caught the fancy of a very uptown woman, but he let her go after a couple of rallies, because, as he said a little ruefully, "I couldn't have afforded to buy her nail polish."

But now, Eric and I have struck North Avenue, at the bottom of a trough—a long groove running east-west from one end of town to the other. To our right, it cuts through Reservoir Hill and Bolton Hill—neighborhoods full of grand stone town houses that have been through a thirty-year decline and are still flirting now with regentrification—and drives to the heart of Baltimore's mostly black and destitute West Side. A terrific target for urban renewal, as the *Baltimore City Paper* pointed out this fall: "Imagine a vibrant boulevard that connects the various halves of Baltimore—East and West, white and black, comfortable and struggling—with movie theaters and music venues, national retailers and local stores alike . . . Can't you just see a healthy artery chugging through the city's torso, spreading wealth and prosperity east and west from the Jones Falls corridor?"

Well, no, you can't, not here, not now . . . except as an agreeable fantasy image floating around in your mind's eye. Eastways, North Avenue terminates at the Baltimore City Cemetery; the moon, which seems to shrink as it rises, hangs cold above its big stone gate. One of my ancestors is buried in there, a slingshot south of the railroad track. He came to Baltimore to die, where no one he knew could see him do it—a stranger in a very strange land to him, lonesome and a long way from home. That northeast corner of the graveyard is usually empty of living beings. The stones are flat to the ground, and often buried under hay left by the mowers. Sometimes I go there to sit and brood. I don't have a lot to say as we cross North Avenue now. Eric, with his own losses to consider, is silent, too.

On the southeast corner is Greenmount Cemetery—white tombstones and mausoleums and stone angels climbing the height of another hillock. The area was still countryside when the ground was consecrated for burials in 1839. Among some sixty-five thousand buried here are John Wilkes Booth, the Confederate general Joe Johnston, poet Sidney Lanier, local tycoons and philanthropists Johns Hopkins and Enoch Pratt, and Betsy Patterson, the Baltimore belle who married Napoléon Bonaparte's brother Jérôme. The Duke and Duchess of

Windsor thought about digging in here, too, but at the last minute changed their minds. Here also eternally reposes Elinor Douglas Wise, Duchesse de Richelieu, who met her duke while taking voice lessons in France, married him in 1913, then further distinguished herself by singing to tubercular French soldiers during World War I and (much later) by becoming a very distant forebear of George W. Bush.

On the east side of Greenmount Avenue, the cemetery's main gate is a humongous pile of brown stone: three Gothic Revival archways, the central one topped with a couple of towers like a pair of rooks on a chessboard. The iron gates under the arches are locked tight, and the stone wall around the plot is serious business, topped with a few extra feet of chain link and barbed wire just to be double sure.

"How do you get in?" says Eric.

"They don't want you to get in," I point out. By day, the cemetery is open to mourners and sightseers alike, but by night, in this neighborhood, it would be a gangbangers' playground. Right now, the curb below the cemetery wall is parked solid with trailers for a sci-fi/horror flick called *The Visiting,* inspired if not based on *Invasion of the Body Snatchers,* and starring the unsinkable Nicole Kidman. Ms. Kidman's lustrous presence in town has created a good deal of rumor and buzz, but she is nowhere to be seen on this block at this hour, and neither is anybody else for that matter—we've got it all to ourselves.

The railroad tracks from Penn Station on Charles Street plunge into a tunnel just to our left. Above it, a row of brick and Formstone houses are very thoroughly boarded up. Looking the other way, west along the cut, we see that the reddening sun is still lingering in this gap of the western skyline. In fact, the rising moon and the setting sun are in the sky at the same time, for whatever that might be worth as an omen. Eric finds the high mansard roof of the Belvedere Hotel, home of Baltimore's famous Owl Bar, picked out by the last brilliant crimson light on the horizon. Since 1903, the Belvedere has towered over Mount Vernon, the wealthy and cultivated downtown neighborhood that furnished Greenmount Cemetery with many of its most distinguished corpses.

By this time, having walked close to five miles at a swinging pace, I am thirsty again. At the top of the next rise, just past the graveyard wall, another oasis appears on the opposite corner: Avenue Liquors and Bar, promising "package goods, ice, open 7 days . . ." I nudge Eric, and we climb the steps and pop into another Plexiglas holding tank, similar to Wozi's in its basic design, though a little larger and better lit. The heavy plastic partitions are so yellowed and scarred you can barely see through them; the Korean cashier on the other side looks blurry as a ghost. There's a black couple ahead of us, clad in matching fuzzy white sweat suits, negotiating their ration of grog. The drill is to lay your money down in the compartment of a Plexiglas lazy Susan that's open to you, while the proprietor places your bottle of choice in the opposite compartment facing him. A quick rotation of the cylinder exchanges payment for goods with next to no compromise of security.

To enter the back-room bar, you must pass a visual inspection. Apparently, Eric and I will do, for after the Korean gentleman gives us a good looking over, he buzzes us through. The bar is atypically bright, with an extension of the cashier's counter cutting a short diagonal across it, and cluttered with cardboard packing cases. Eric and I about fill the place up. Behind the counter is an array of little airline liquor bottles on a small set of shelves, and a glass-front refrigerator full of beer. But the owner is still serving street-side customers through the lazy Susan to our left.

A hand-lettered sign over an open door way in back reads MAN. That looks hopeful to me, so I climb a couple of steps and go through. At once a woman bolts upright from a cot in a shadowy alcove to my left, whipping her head as she winds her sheet more tightly about her—surprised as she is, she doesn't make a sound, and neither do I as I blunder on, through relative darkness and a couple of doors, till in fact I do find an operational toilet. By the time I get back, which is not very long, the woman I roused has morphed into a barmaid, is serving Eric his drink, and seems to be the nicest young Korean lady you'd ever want to meet.

The Korean owner might be about our age (which is, alas, late forties) or maybe a little older (or younger, who knows). Smiling, he asks if we are here on business, which I know has got to mean he's wondering what the hell kind of business we could possibly have around here. When I tell him we are walking lower Greenmount Avenue just for the sheer fun of it, his expression goes opaque and he slides back behind his cash register, around the corner and out of our sight. Not to ask too many questions is a courtesy, I sense. Eric and I drink our beer and talk a little college shop, which must seem fairly bizarre to our barmaid, who listens (or doesn't listen) with her smile fixed firmly on her face and her eyes sinking almost shut.

Korean stores in black slum neighborhoods are a long-established paradigm here. Typically, the Koreans are in these neighborhoods without being of them—and the security system here at Avenue Liquors suggests that it is no exception (though black-run operations like Wozi's use much the same series of safeguards as here). During the riots in Los Angeles in the 1990s, we saw the same kind of Korean entrepreneurs returning fire on black rioters from the roofs of their shops. This determined self-defense, or vigilantism, or whatever you want to call it, was applauded by everyone at Master Lee's tae kwon do school (which I was still attending at the time) . . . including me.

Koreans were latecomers in New York and Los Angeles and other major cities, where they followed earlier

waves of Asian immigration—but they were the first
Asians in Baltimore, and they have been here for a long
time. Korea is a small, proud, and intransigent country
with centuries worth of bad relations with both Japan
and China. Baltimore had next-to-no Japanese or Chinese populations when the Koreans began to arrive in
large numbers during the 1970s, when South Korean
president Park Chung Hee opened an immigration door
by way of his support of U.S. military efforts in Vietnam.
My two tae kwon do masters, Young I Lee and Chung
Sik Park, washed in on this 1970s immigration wave.
There was still work enough in Baltimore's industrial
parks to attract them. Before his group's arrival here,
Master Park has told me, there were only three or four
hundred Koreans in Baltimore, many of them professional people, or students at Johns Hopkins University.

New Korean arrivals not working in the industrial
sector started laundries and dry cleaners and restaurants—
usually Chinese or Japanese restaurants, since these
cuisines were more familiar to Baltimore round eyes.
Until quite recently, it was safe to assume that any Chinese or Japanese restaurant here was staffed by Koreans
(ironically enough), but lately a few purely Korean eateries have opened up (Purim Oak in Towson, Nam Kang
in Lower Charles Village . . . and I have a feeling the Yellow Bowl noodle shop, adjoining Avenue Liquors, is
probably another of these, run by the same family).
Locals who cultivate a taste for kimchi, the fiery Korean

pickled cabbage, can now get it homemade in neighborhood Asian groceries.

For a time, Baltimore boasted several small newspapers printed in hangul, but more recently these have been overtaken by Internet news, national publications in Korean, and free newsletters distributed by the several churches dominated by Korean Christians. Now there are some thirty-five thousand Koreans in the Baltimore area, and about half of them inside the city limits; Koreans are the largest minority in Baltimore, after blacks—who can hardly be called a minority in Baltimore, where they amount to 64.3 percent of the population.

Korean-black clashes have been notorious in other inner cities around the United States. In Baltimore, though some of the same tensions do exist, they don't seem to come to a violent head. The Avenue Liquors family is bound to be on its way through and up—the next generation may well be attending the Johns Hopkins University medical school, even as we speak.

We're cordially offered another drink but figure it is time to go. Back in the air-lock region of the store, it's suddenly crowded and a little rowdy. The customers have begun to consume the product. It's getting seriously dark outside. Before we step back into the street, I tie a camouflage bandanna around my head, which I figure may enhance my anonymity, at a distance in bad light.

South of Preston Street, every corner's got a camera— a boxy little thing raised on a high pole like a martin house. My first guess is that these must be some of those detested red-light cameras, but Eric pegs them as surveillance cameras, lately installed in the most violent areas of town . . . of which this must be one, I infer. Supposedly (I learn when I look them up later), these cameras can pan, tilt, zoom, and practically look down your throat . . . but somehow I don't *feel* that they're doing any of these things, and the people milling around in the next few blocks don't seem tremendously impressed by them, either. Is Big Brother really watching? There wouldn't be a whole hell of a lot for him to see—just a couple of middle-aged white guys stepping out quickly past rows of mostly boarded-up brick housefronts.

Off to our right appear in the gloaming the dreary Victorian fortifications of the old Maryland Penitentiary, whose first structures have stood on this ground since the early nineteenth century. From 1811 to 1879, it was the only prison in the state—receiving all malefactors, including women, juveniles, and the criminally insane, and until quite recently it remained the state system's highest security prison, colloquially known as the "Supermax." It's located, oddly enough, no more than a hop, skip, or jump from Baltimore's once most fashionable neighborhood, Mount Vernon. From where we're walking on Greenmount Avenue, Eric and I can look past the dour turrets of the prison and glimpse the statue of George Washington standing high on the 178-foot stone column that Melville described, in *Moby Dick,* as a "towering main mast," in the center of Mount Vernon Place. A century back, the Jones Falls stream made a natural barrier between the prison and posh Mount Vernon; nowadays, the stream runs underground in this part of town, and the divide is marked by the ramp of the Jones Falls Expressway, the southernmost tip of I-83, as it makes its final descent to downtown street level and the harbor.

In those good old days, the gentlefolk of Mount Vernon and like neighborhoods would sometimes cast a curious eye in the direction of the prison. In 1818, John Duncan watched the hanging of two mail robbers in the prison yard. "I had in my pocket a small perspective glass which I offered to two young ladies who happened to stand near me; they seemed quite pleased with the accommodation and continued to use it alternately till the whole melancholy scene was over." Executions continued here into the 1990s, though in 1923 they were moved indoors and ceased to be a public spectacle, and the method evolved from the gallows through the gas chamber to lethal injection. Though Maryland does still have the death penalty, it has seldom been exercised since the 1960s. In 1998, after the move of maximum security inmates to a new facility south of town, the old prison was reorganized as the Metropolitan Transition Center, more commonly known as Central Booking, and now houses short-timers only, typically defendants awaiting trial. As we pass by one of the more recent additions to the complex, we catch a view through a clouded window of half a dozen black men, responding to some invisible order, shuffling into a loose rank, blinking in harsh fluorescent light, their shoulders slack and their heads hanging low.

Greenmount Avenue disintegrates into a nerve center of crisscrossing highways, fanning away from downtown. Off to our west, the Jones Falls Expressway is making its final approach to terra firma. We're surrounded now by nondescript institutional buildings of the late twentieth century—an old Jewish neighborhood was razed to put them here, Eric thinks. A zig and a zag brings us onto a corner dominated by the Baltimore City Fire Museum at 414 North Gay Street—the street number echoing firebox 414, which was the first alarm pulled to announce the devastating Great Baltimore Fire of 1904. A firehouse has stood on this corner for more than two hundred years, its engine bay topped by a three-stage, redbrick clock and bell tower in the style of an Italian campanile.

The 1904 fire began near the corner of Liberty and Lombard Street and blazed its way to the west bank of the Jones Falls stream, burning the Pratt Street docks to the waterline and, in the course of twenty-four hours, destroying practically all of Baltimore-Town, as it was originally laid out in 1729. Thirty-seven fire engines closed ranks along the banks of the Jones Falls and successfully stopped the fire from jumping the stream into Little Italy and Old Town, where it might have continued to roar eastward across Canton and Fells Point. Today, the ground where we walk has been cleared not by fire but by progress; the old firehouse is a quaint little island dividing the asphalt streams of Highways 147 and 40. Across the way, a billboard makes a wicked visual pun— over a stylized image of Deborah Kerr and Burt Lancaster thrashing in the surf is a banner headline: "FROM HERE TO **PA**TERNITY—DNA TESTING."

We keep cutting west. On the north side of Fayette Street, a white bullet-shaped tower rises from the modest church of Saint Vincent de Paul. In the side garden, under the trees south of the church, is a semipermanent encampment of the homeless, with blanket shelters and tarpaulins strung up against the weather. A few people resting there are barely visible, in darkness and deep shade. Saint Vincent de Paul has followed a mission to bring help to Baltimore's unhoused poor since 1865. The little camp in the grove of old trees has the air of sanctuary, a deep calm.

At the corner of Fayette and North Front Street, the Phoenix Shot Tower rises, a dense redbrick cone 234 feet high—the tallest building in the United States when it was raised in 1828. In those days, shot manufacturers dropped hot lead from the top to pass through perforated pans midway. Rounded to perfect spheres in their long descent, the droplets plunged into cold water at the bottom and hardened into shotgun pellets. Charles Carroll, a signer of the American Declaration of Independence who used to winter with his family in an elegant brick mansion a block or two south, laid the Shot Tower's cornerstone.

Since 1768, the Carrolls had been major landholders in Maryland. Alexis de Tocqueville, who met Charles Carroll in the 1830s, noted that in signing the Declaration, Carroll "risked, together with his life, the most considerable fortune that there was in America." Charles Carroll bought what is now known as the Carroll Mansion for his daughter Mary and her husband, and finally died there, after fourteen winters in the city. A regimen that included a five-mile horseback ride, a daily bath (unusual in Carroll's day), and the avoidance of highly seasoned foods that might "excite the passions" allowed him to live to the age of ninety-five. His heirs eventually let the mansion go. A tenement by the end of the nineteenth century, it later housed a furniture store, a vocational school, and, in the 1940s, Baltimore's first recreational center. Vacant and derelict, it narrowly escaped demolition in 1956, and stands today as a centerpiece of the Baltimore City Life Museum system.

We cut across the tiny green apron surrounding the Shot Tower and head south on Front Street. To the west, the sky is a deep velvet blue. The Jones Falls emerges from its invisible passage under President Street, and flows a few blocks farther south to join the Northwest Branch of the Patapsco River in the Inner Harbor. A humongous balloon is tethered to the ground in front of Port Discovery, where the old fish market was remodeled into a children's museum and recreation center in 1998. Daytime, the balloon goes up and down like an elevator, packed with merrily shrieking kids.

We're looking for more grown-up fun tonight. Passing the escalator for the Shot Tower stop on Baltimore's solitary subway line, we cross a wide expanse of cobblestones and enter an iron fence that encloses both the Carroll Mansion and the former City Life Museum Exhibition Center, rejuvenated in 2004 as Gardel's, an Argentine dance and supper club. The building, raised by the Fava Fruit company in 1869, has a four-story, bloodred cast-iron facade that looks something like a gigantic layer cake. Cast-iron facades were all the rage in Baltimore once upon a time, facing more than a hundred buildings around town; Gardel's has one of only a few that remain today.

We swing through the revolving doors and cross the softly gleaming dance floor, headed for the bar. Overhead, blown-glass mobiles shimmer softly in the vast reaches of the ceiling. A giant photo of Carlos Gardel, elegant in a snap-brim Panama, surveys the scene from the western wall. Gardel, an Argentine crooner who in the 1920s had the notion of adding lyrics to the heretofore instrumental music of the tango, is the tutelary spirit of the club.

It's early yet, just 7:30, and Gardel's only has its first few dinner guests. Sleek in their black shirts and slacks, the staff flickers through the opulent shadows, setting up.

A few booths along the back wall have already been staked for Salsa Night. Shannon, the bar manager, is traveling at mach speed behind the counter, making ready for the throngs that will pack the place later, her focus tight and her movement slicingly efficient. We've been perched on our stools for not quite two minutes when she picks up her beautiful blond head and sees us there.

Her eyes widen for a second when I tell her the route we just walked. "What would you want to do that for?" I feel a little bit like an eight-year-old boy trying to impress a girl with a frog, in that I can't quite make out if she thinks we are daring, crazy, or just really dumb. It's slow yet in the bar, though, so we lure Shannon out to have a quick drink with us at an iron table on the 1840s Plaza, which Gardel's and the Carroll Mansion share.

The fat disk of the harvest moon gets smaller and brighter as it clears the roof behind us. The traffic floating down President Street is hushed in this pocket where we sit. Shannon is quiet. She's leaving Gardel's. In a year's time, she'll be running her own place in Highlandtown, the Laughing Pint, where the regulars look at her, without irony, like she was some kind of guardian angel. But she doesn't know that yet. Just as she gets up to go back to work, a wedding party comes through the gate, bound for the 1840s Ballroom on the fourth floor. Under the moon (and the spotlight of their videographer), bride and groom do a slow pas de deux to the languorous Latin music rippling from Gardel's outdoor speakers. Lives are changing all around us. We may not know it, but they are.

"If I were ten years younger," Eric says; he might be talking about a lot of things.

Johnny Alonso appears at our table—the oldest of the three sons referred to in the name of Gardel's management team, "Doctor Alonso and Sons." In fact there are two Doctors Alonso—he a Spaniard, she a Filipina. When not practicing medicine, they both dance the tango. The club is the fruit of their love for the dance. Tango enthusiasts from a long way back, they began giving lessons at Baltimore's Creative Alliance. When they got a chance to take over this amazing space, they took it. Robert Duvall, star of *Assassination Tango* (among other films), has shared the Alonsos' tango craze for years, and was one of the guests of honor when the club opened in 2004.

The Alonsos' middle son, James, a writer, musician, and daytime contractor, organized the remodeling of the vacant, slightly crumbling Exhibition Center into a sleek three floors of nightclub, doing much of its very loving craftsmanship with his own hands. He built the dance floor, working the wood into a preexisting pattern of black-and-white tiles, and he has rearranged all the partitions, and, in fact, he is still doing detail work on the place, more or less whenever it's not open to the public. His approach has a rough-and-ready ingenuity: He will cannibalize the iron legs of warped tables for the posts of an interior balcony, or surface a bar with scraps of veneer from the nearby Paul Reed Smith guitar-maker's shop. Every time I come, there's something new: a display case, a wall ornamented with stained glass. Some of the museum features on the second floor have been preserved for the club—a working replica of a White Tower lunch counter, and three historical murals: Howard Street in its heyday as a high-end shopping district; a footrace in Patterson Park, past the weird elevation of the pagoda-style tower there; and (perhaps most suitably for the present-day club) a night street scene with a marquee featuring the Cab Calloway orchestra. The Gardel's crew has added a bar, a couple of pool tables, and a set of poufy black leather couches and armchairs that produces an interesting visual reverberation with the black-and-chrome revolving stools of the lunch counter.

The third floor has the office space; James keeps meaning to build himself an apartment up there but hasn't quite got around to it yet. There's a big room there for private parties; James built the bar and the DJ booth. James plays bass sometimes for a band of mine that sometimes exists, and the Gardel's third floor is a great place to practice at the end of the day, under the wall of west-facing windows, with the crimson light gilding all our gear as the sun sinks over the Baltimore skyline.

Since the club opened, James shares the management with Johnny and the youngest Alonso son, Jason. Johnny's an actor, when not running the club. A regular on *Dawson's Creek* until that show ended, lately he's been doing guest spots on *One Tree Hill*. Back in the day, he was guitarist and singer for the Unknown, a local band in which James played bass. At Gardel's, he deejays and masterminds special events; right now, he's brewing a plan to bring Nicole Kidman here for a special treat.

Bursting full-blown from the Alonso brain, Gardel's is now one of the very best restaurants in Baltimore. I just walked around six miles, Eric better than four. We go inside and snag a table. Both of us get the tortilla soup. I follow up with Sofrito Marinated Grilled Loin of Pork, with Goat Cheese Creamed Mote de Maiz, Grilled Endive, Chipotle Papaya Chutney, and clean that plate, thank you very much, while Eric gets the osso buco. The Gardel's wine list is fantastic. Sadly, neither one of us can quite find room for a dessert.

James has been MIA since we got here, maybe en route from his house in North Baltimore, maybe somewhere in the back rooms or upper levels of the club. When I ask James how he's doing these days, he tells me, "I'm steering a really big boat." Eric has been getting updates on a device which looks to me like a small Game Boy or DVD player, but which he claims is a cell phone.

Live and in person, James rolls up to our table just in time to stop us from sinking into a postprandial stupor. Beth, our waitress, takes that as a cue to unpin her surprisingly long auburn hair and sit down with us for a drink. She's a portrait painter on her own time, we learn, and took the job at Gardel's (which is generally a big employer of the moonlighting Baltimore arts community) because it gives her plenty of time to paint. She likes Steiner's idea that painting makes it impossible to lie, and she prefers painting adults when she can, because "they cannot guard themselves from a painter. Whatever it may be that they are holding back reveals itself whether they like it or not." But she gets more commissions to paint children, since people are more willing to have their children painted than themselves, and she likes painting children well enough, though it's a bit less of a challenge since children are naturally more open . . .

Her friend Christopher, elegant in a tailored-looking suit, floats on the edge of the conversation, frequently getting up to dance. He's a sculptor and ex-pro ballroom dancer, and he and Beth first discovered Gardel's for tango, before she started working here. They definitely came to the right place. The atmosphere of the club is shifting into second gear. Saturday is Salsa Night at Gardel's, and the music is just beginning to throb. Alone on the dance floor appears a girl with bobbed blond hair and a tight black minidress—she cocks up her spike heel behind her, kicks down and spins away, expertly twirled in the hands of her partner, a tall, lean young man who might be gawky if he wasn't dancing, who would be way too tall for her if they weren't dancing—but the grace of their movement makes them a perfect match. For a few minutes, they are alone in the spotlight of everyone else's rapt attention, and then a few more couples glide onto the floor, and then the salsa lesson that's been happening on the second floor lets out, and all of a sudden the dance floor is full, and the tables are full, and the whole place is booming.

"Hey," says Eric, and I follow his eyes to a tall and rangy, sharp-looking blond, coming up from the back wall of the big room.

"I think I know that woman."

"We both do," I say. Elise is a Goucher graduate, and was one of my best fiction students back in the day. She makes her living working with horses, and for the past few years she's been doing Latin dance, which helps limber her up after long days in the saddle. She's a show-horse trainer nowadays, though she also schooled steeplechasers for a fun-filled couple of years, and her current day job is running a stable in the hunt country north of town, where she lives with her Siberian husky, a barn full of high-class horseflesh, and a nicer gun collection than usual for a college-educated woman.

I wave, and we pull her a chair at our table. Elise has been coming to Salsa Night at Gardel's since it opened. Tonight is the first time she's going to dance in those high heels she's got in that little bag slung over her shoulder— says she's a little nervous about it, too. For some time, I've nursed a secret desire to learn the tango. Tonight's salsa dancing is supposed to be easier, and Elise, whirling around in her slim black trousers and brilliant white sequined top, does make it look easy, high heels or no.

People tell Elise that she dances like a Latina, which seems believable enough to my eyes, and Elise thinks that salsa isn't *easier* than the tango but *freer* than the tango. "Light, fun, and complicated" says she. A couple of rums, and I feel like maybe I could give it a try. I think I wasn't properly listening to the complicated part of the description.

Elise taught my daughter to ride horses, while I watched, and I know her to be a wise and patient instructor—the only problem is I am a far less apt student than she's used to or deserves. Though I don't know it, she is actually trying to simplify my situation by teaching me the cha-cha, a step alleged to be still easier than salsa, though not quite easy enough for me. Twenty minutes on the floor and I am washed in a sickly sweat, breathless and feeling pretty thoroughly dislocated from the hips on down. Elise would never give up on me—no!—but her smile is getting a little fixed, and the instructional mantra (One! Two! Cha-cha-cha!) is coming out more stiffly from between her teeth. Moreover, I think I have been trampling her unfortunate feet more than I should . . . and I somehow suspect that she would be willing for me to give up on myself, at least temporarily, if I should have the good sense to do that.

So I go back to the bench and leave her to dance with more competent partners, of which there is no shortage. The floor is jamfull by this time and more people keep pouring in from the courtyard. Crowded like that, it's no place for klutzes. Some of the best dancers, like Beth's friend Christopher and that first skillful couple, have moved out into the area around the stairwell and the hostesses podium, where they can have more room.

City life! If Charles Carroll was still occupying his house on the corner, he'd probably be beefing about the noise, but this is a different style of American Dream than any of the Founding Fathers would have dreamed up: a rainbow of every shade on the broad spectrum of Baltimore citizenry, black and Latin and Asian and white, all dressed to the nines and ready to dance with the friends they know, or with beautiful and graceful strangers who by the end of the evening may be strangers no more. Sure, there's a dose of security here, as there has to be at any club that draws so many people from all across the city map, but it's invisibly discreet. If any trouble begins to brew, it gets neutralized and dissipated before anyone has the slightest clue it was ever trying to get started. And all these people are pulled into harmony, at least for the time that they are here, by the music and the dance, while iridescent bubbles of blown glass above all tremble and sway with that good-feeling vibe.

Doctor and Doctor Alonso swing through, meeting and greeting, sparkling in their evening clothes, though they probably won't do much dancing tonight: Tango is their passion, not salsa so much, and Tango Night is Tuesday. When they have passed on, Elise makes a controlled crash landing at our table, flushed and glowing—

she's been out on the floor for about an hour, so you'd have to call the shoe debut a success. But now she rips off her heels without much ceremony, groans (but daintily), and slips on a pair of soft black flats.

So now I get a chance to discover that my problem catching on to salsa has nothing to do with whatever shoes Elise is wearing, and that the rum I drank since my last try doesn't even make me think I'm dancing better now. The *back*bone connected to the *hip* bone, the *hip* bone connected to the *thigh*bone, the *thigh*bone connected to the *knee* bone, the *knee* bone connected to the *shin*bone, the *shin*bone connected to the *ankle*bone, the *ankle*bone connected to the *foot* bone—and all these connections are letting me know how far I have walked this evening. It's one in the morning, and people are still pouring into Gardel's like they're being washed in on a waterfall. It will be hopping here for quite some time longer, but when I run into somebody who's driving my way, I jump at the ride.

Dickeyville

O N THE SUNDAY MORNING OF THANKSGIVING
weekend, I drive from Cedarcroft across downtown Baltimore, skirting the western rim of the Inner
Harbor, southbound on Light Street, and continue into
Federal Hill, which isn't a neighborhood I know tremendously well. Federal Hill proper, a big, square, grassy
berm with a pleasant park on top, drops away to my left
as I keep rolling south. John Smith (yes, that's Pocahon-
tas's John Smith) described it as a great red bank of clay
flanking a natural harbor when he came sailing up the
Patapsco in 1609, and before American independence it
was known as "John Smith's Hill." Two centuries later,
some three thousand people gathered there to celebrate
the ratification of the U.S. Constitution by Maryland.

If you climb one of the several staircases to the top
of the hill, you can treat yourself to a panoramic view
across the crooked fingertip of the Patapsco River that is

Baltimore's Inner Harbor, bustling on weekends especially with water taxis and other pleasure craft ferrying
tourists to the Maryland Science Center or the National
Aquarium at Baltimore or to Fells Point or all the way
out to Fort McHenry at the harbor's mouth. Across the
water, you will see the glass and steel of Baltimore's downtown renascence—hotel and convention centers spreading their glittering fingers into the sky. Francis Scott Key
didn't stand exactly here to watch "the rockets red glare"
and "bombs bursting in air"; he collected the raw material from the famously unsingable "Star-Spangled Banner"
from the deck of a ship nearer Fort McHenry—but your
perspective from the top of Federal Hill would be similar
enough to his.

For more than a century after the battle Key immor-
talized, the Inner Harbor was a busy working port. By
the mid-twentieth century, it had gone into a deep
enough decline that one sour-minded observer described
it as "the chief dead lady of East Coast cities." In the late
1970s, the Rouse Company (later responsible for New
York's South Street Seaport), rehabbed the area as an
open-air mall. Since then, the Inner Harbor has been one
of Baltimore's strongest tourist attractions and a pleasant
place for locals as well.

Federal Hill, the neighborhood, rolls softly down the
slope south of the Federal Hill park, through block after
block of the classic Baltimore row houses, most of these
built in the nineteenth century, small but comfy two- or

three-story bricks, each with a set of the white stone steps, which old-school Baltimoreans are renowned for scrubbing to a dazzling gleam. I keep on cruising south on Light Street. This early on a Sunday morning, I just about have it all to myself. The only disadvantage is next-to-no parking, since nobody has yet budged their cars.

I find a place on Fort Street (so called because it runs a couple of miles east to Fort McHenry) and, since I'm early for my rendezvous, I walk a couple of blocks farther south and take a loop through Riverside Park, empty except for a few early dog walkers, green and calm with a distant view of the water to the east. By the time I return to Fort Street, churchgoers have started to circulate. I head a couple of blocks north, to pick up Laura Lippman.

Laura and David Simon have an unusual but perhaps ideal arrangement for a writer couple. They met as reporters on the *Baltimore Sun*. Simon, who was well on the way to converting his nonfiction book *Homicide* into the first of several hit TV series he's written since, had recently moved into a converted church in Federal Hill. Laura, herself a novelist then best known for her Tess Monaghan mystery series, bought the house next door, which happens to have been the parsonage. Thanks to this arrangement, they can live together and still have plenty of private workspace.

Following Laura's directions, I hop on the Key Highway, hook around to I-95, and go south to the westbound ramp of the Baltimore Beltway. We drive roughly from six to nine o'clock on the dial, and get off on I-70, which heads back into the city, though not for long. When Laura used to tell someone how to find her childhood home in Dickeyville, she began by saying, "Go east on I-70 till it ends," whereupon the prospective visitor would disbelievingly object, since in theory interstate highways go on and on forever. As originally planned, I-70 was supposed to slash all the way southeast across Baltimore, cutting a swathe through the Federal Hill neighborhood where Laura lives now—but protests from the threatened neighborhoods stopped it. Now the highway dribbles off into a so-called Park and Ride, with maybe fiftysome parking spots. Another triumph of the Baltimore public transit system, I quip as we pass it by. That system is charmingly unsystematic, featuring a subway with just one line (it runs from Johns Hopkins Hospital and the Phoenix Shot Tower downtown on a northwest diagonal out to Owings Mills) and a light rail train that shuttles a very few passengers between BWI airport, Camden Yards, a handful of downtown stations, and a few select northeast neighborhoods.

Laura left the *Sun* a few years back, following the trail David Simon had blazed away from the paper, which has never been entirely hospitable to its reporters writing books on their own time. But she was a perceptive and wide-ranging reporter in her day (twelve years at the *Sun*); she saw a lot and forgot very little. The Tess

Monaghan mysteries, along with the "stand-alone" novels she's been writing recently, are saturated in her broad and deep knowledge of Baltimore neighborhoods and communities. The first of these that she knew was Dickeyville. When she was six years old, she moved there with her family from Northern Virginia; her father, Theo Lippman Jr., had just taken a job as an editorial writer at the *Sun*.

I-70's grand aspirations take a nosedive into a gravel bank at the western end of Leakin Park. We turn away and head northeast on Forest Park Avenue, which turns out to be closed to all but local traffic, thanks to construction on a bridge. But we are local traffic, so we press on as far as Wetheredsville Road, where I turn south and coast down the steepish hill of Dickeyville's main drag, whose curves echo the windings of the Gwynn's Falls stream. We cruise by Ashland Chapel, built in the 1830s for a Quaker meetinghouse and later converted into a Methodist church. A bit farther down, we pass the whitewashed stone building built in 1832 as a school for Dickeyville millworkers' children: A small bronze medallion fixed between red shutters presents a small image of a hastening scholar who might be worried about being late. Then the houses peter out, and just beyond a hairpin turn, we stop and park beside the mill.

Richard Gwynn came here in 1672 to trade with the Algonquin Indians. In 1719, Gwynn's son-in-law Peter Bond built a water mill on the stream that became known as the Gwynn's Falls. Around this enterprise, a small community began to grow and prosper—ten years before Baltimore Town, seven miles southeast on a backwater of the Patapsco River, first received its charter. In 1762, Wimbert Tschudi built a gristmill on the stream. In 1811, the Franklin Paper Mill was constructed a short distance up the creek. A year later, Dickeyville dwellings served as emergency hospitals for American soldiers wounded while fighting off the British at the battles of North Point and Fort McHenry.

In 1829, John Wethered bought the Franklin Paper Mill and converted it to cloth, and the village took on his name. He also added a new mill complex at the lower end of present-day Wetheredsville Road. Cotton and wool clothing from the Wethered Mills became widely appreciated all over the country, and during the Civil War, the family is thought to have had a profitable business selling uniforms to the Confederate army. Disaster also came their way: a fire that destroyed a complex known as Ashland Mills in 1854, and then, in 1857, the bursting of the Powhatan Dam upstream did a hundred thousand dollars worth of damage. In 1863, the Union army confiscated the whole mill complex, and the Wethered family lost its grip on the industry and the community. Twelve years later, following some legal wrangling with the Wethereds, the Dickey family acquired at auction a tract of three hundred acres surrounding three mills and their now-numerous outbuildings; from then on, the village was called Dickeyville.

There is a tremendous amount of water in, around, and underneath Baltimore. The Gwynn's Falls starts somewhere north of town and flows down through Sudbrook Park and Villa Nova Park and the vast Woodlawn Cemetery, south of Liberty Road. At the south end of Woodlawn Cemetery, the stream is dammed to form a small, fishhook-shaped lake, but there is plenty of water left to drive the mills at Dickeyville and drop down farther south into Leakin Park. The Jones Falls comes into town from the north, along Falls Road, and is dammed, just northwest of where I live in Cedarcroft, to form Lake Roland in Robert E. Lee Park, then keeps on spilling south of the dam, followed in its course by both railroad track and the Jones Falls Expressway, bordering the North Baltimore neighborhoods—Mount Washington, Roland Park—until it goes underground just south of Hampden, where in bygone days it powered another mill village. This stretch is popular with whitewater kayakers, and features a number of rapids and waterfalls, and legend has it that a couple of careless paddlers got swept into the tunnel in the neighborhood of Forty-first Street and emerged alive, if more than a little shaken, in the Inner Harbor a couple of miles south. Stony Run comes into town east of the Jones Falls, wiggles its way through the elite private school campuses at the edge of Roland Park (Gilman, Bryn Mawr, Roland Park Country School, and Friends), winds through Wyman Park, and finally joins the Jones Falls on its underground passage to the Inner Harbor. Chinquapin Run makes its way through a skinny little park of the same name in Govans, then hooks to the east to join Herring Run as it flows out of Towson and corkscrews its way southeast, passing through a couple of vast industrial parks on its very indirect way to the Patapsco River.

From the beginning, all this water has proved a mixed blessing. In the eighteenth and early nineteenth century, much of Baltimore and its outlying areas were one big malarial swamp—maps from that period show mosquito-borne illness fanning out along most the tributary streams from the Patapsco. Baltimore required two hundred bridges in its early days. Later, swamps were drained and the ground leveled, and many streams channeled underground. When the Jones Falls went under, a speechmaker quipped, "I have come to bury the Jones Falls, not to praise it." Some subsequent construction problems derive from the fact that no one quite remembers now just where all those little creeks were interred. Surprise sinkholes open up downtown, and the solitary subway tunnel is wont to flood near Lombard Street. Lately, there has been a trend in other cities to "daylight" buried streams, and the Baltimore City Department of Public Works is contemplating digging up a few here. Of course, you can have too much of a good thing: When Hurricane Isabel came by in 2003, there was so much open water in Baltimore that people were canoeing through downtown streets near the waterfront. Today's city planners have no intention to take it quite that far.

The Dickeyville stretch of the Gwynn's Falls has always been open to the light of day; it purls to our left as Laura and I descend the path beside it. We don't have the perfect day for a walk—it's overcast and sort of damp, though warmer than it was Thanksgiving Day. Laura's wearing jeans and a pair of maroon gloves and a blue Colts windbreaker with the number *34* in bold white on the back, framed by the logo **COLTS CORRALS**, the fan club back in the glory days when the Colts were the *Baltimore* team. She leads our way downstream on Wetheredsville Road, which has been closed to vehicles past the mill, and rededicated as a footpath.

There are no other walkers today, and drifts of fallen leaves have mostly hidden the worn asphalt. To our right, a sizable tract of woods runs up the hill. To our left, the Gwynn's Falls purls, kicking up a little froth around the stones. When Laura was a kid here in the sixties, she and her friends were warned to keep well away from the stream—because of pollution—though there were crayfish in those days. I point out that she couldn't have been much of a rule follower if she knew about the crayfish. Laura laughs and admits that all the neighborhood kids played in the Gwynn's Falls every warm day, though threatened with tetanus shots if they so much as wet a toe in it.

The path is a gentle descent beside the stream, but it goes a long way down the ravine. We follow it as far as Windsor Mill Road. Beyond, the trail continues south along the boundary between Leakin and Gwynn's Falls Park, to the point where the Gwynn's Falls stream meets another called Dead Run; from there, the Gwynn's Falls keeps winding and widening its way south until it dumps into the Middle Branch of the Patapsco. The trail we're walking is actually fourteen miles long, and since June of 2005 has been open to hikers all the way from the northern city limit to the streams outlet on the Middle Branch, connecting two thousand acres of parkland, and more than thirty neighborhoods along the way, neighborhoods that run the full spectrum from nice to nasty and back again.

The Gwynn's Falls Trail is a reincarnation of a one-hundred-year-old plan—presented to Baltimore in 1904 by John and Frederick Law Olmsted Jr. The great fire that destroyed downtown the same year soaked up all the available public works funding, and the Olmsted plan for a slender park in the Gwynn's Falls gorge was abandoned. In 1999, Chris Rogers, an intern with the Baltimore Parks and People Foundation, rediscovered the plan and was eventually able to get it adopted by the Trust for Public Land. What walkers on the trail most commonly testify is "You won't believe you're in Baltimore City."

The Olmsteds were early advocates of preserving green space within cities, and luckily there is enough parkland within the Baltimore city limits for their ideas to be profitably resurrected. Much of this green space follows the streambeds. There's a ribbon of green along Stony Run that starts at Wyndhurst Avenue in Homeland and runs, with a couple of short interruptions, south to the bottom of Wyman Park at Twenty-ninth Street in Remington. To the east, Herring Run Park flanks the stream of that name from the south side of the Morgan State University campus all the way down to I-895. The Olmsted brothers' plan of 1904 called for *all* the city's fifty-seven hundred acres of green space to be connected by paths along the stream banks. Urban development during the hundred years since has raised a few obstacles to the dormant Olmsted project, but in recent years the city government has taken serious steps toward putting those old ideas into practice. The Gwynn's Falls Trail is the longest to be completed so far; meanwhile, there are plans to connect the slim green space along Chinquapin Run with Clifton Park to the east, and thence to Herring Run Park. A more ambitious greenway project will open ten miles of trail along the Jones Falls, from Lake Roland through Druid Hill Park to the downtown "Cultural District" of Mount Vernon, linking twenty extremely diverse neighborhoods along the way.

When we're done with our Dickeyville exploration, I drive Laura home by way of Windsor Mill Road and Gwynn's Falls Parkway and Druid Park Lake Drive—the latter road skirting Druid Hill Park, named in honor of the ancient oaks in its old-growth forest. The flora of Druid Hill and Leakin Park have been left for the most part unmolested since the city was founded. Druid Hill Park is also home to the Cylburn Arboretum, along with the Maryland Zoo in Baltimore and its adjacent Reptile House, the latter building just recently closed. The area around the Reptile House, Laura tells me as we whiz by, used to be a well-known cruising ground for gay men, one of whom would occasionally turn up dead in the surrounding shrubbery—and on the southeast edge of this park is a big man-made lake with a fountain where the body of a thirty-five-year-old woman was found in 1969; three decades later, her case is still open. Laura has a mystery writer's eye for corpses, but that's not all, and as we leave Druid Hill Park behind she embarks on another story (which she and Simon are writing up as a movie script). One Malsby, a once-distinguished *Sun* reporter on his last legs, used to do his daytime drinking at the zoo, where he formed a sympathetic relationship with a gorilla named Baltimore Jack, whose abiding sorrow was that he had never got laid, which predicament Malsby turned into a cause célèbre and his last major series of stories for the *Sun*—until a suitable lady gorilla (yclept Hazel) was found for Baltimore Jack in Arizona, but still the simian lovers stars were crossed because Maryland governor Marvin Mandel wouldn't permit state funds to be used to transport Baltimore Jack to Chicago (which was hypocritical of him, Laura points out, since during the same period he was using his state-funded security detail to convey him back and forth from *his* mistress's house), so finally Hugh Hefner volunteered his Playboy jet to fly the frustrated gorilla to meet his inamorata at the Arizona Zoo, during which flight he was chained to a bed, which, for some reason (guess if you can) was already part of the Playboy jet furnishings . . .

. . . but we are not done with Dickeyville yet. At Windsor Mill Road, we double back and start climbing the hill the way we came. Both of us are stiff and sore from the previous day—I was doing push-hands with my neighbor, Dangerous Doctor Geoff (a tai chi and swai jiao expert in his spare time), and Laura was playing touch football with David Simon and his son Ethan—so a little effort going uphill warms and limbers us up a little, and that is a good thing. Laura has long legs and a determined stride and is in the habit of walking from Federal Hill to the Charles Theatre or once in a while to Viva House, the soup kitchen where she volunteers in the Hollins Market area—both around five miles round-trip. I keep pace with her back to the concrete pad where I parked my car across from the mill. We cross a bridge over the stream into the mill compound—when Laura was a child, a cotton thread mill was still operating here, but that's been over for quite a while, and now the long, two-story whitewashed stone and brick building has been converted to office space for Allied Medical and All in One Granite & Marble and roughly a dozen more businesses.

West of the Gwynn's Falls again, we cut into a strip of woods, and soon emerge onto a wide greensward behind the houses facing Wetheredsville Road. This area is, officially, a park, and a few people have set up Adirondack chairs on the high bank above the stream. On the ridge opposite, through the mostly bare branches of the autumn trees, we can see a few houses in Windsor Hills—a prosperous black suburb when Laura was a kid. Across Wetheredsville Road on the other side, we can see the house where she grew up—a pleasant three-story duplex behind a white picket fence, with the redbrick walls beginning to show through naturally distressed white paint.

At a dogleg of the stream, there's a small clear gravel-bottomed pool, with a dear little wooden sign marked SALAMANDER WAY—Laura says she never found any salamanders here as a kid, though there used to be some around the springhouse whose foundations are still standing, near the bottom of the wooded slope across Wetheredsville Road. Today, a little clear water still drizzles through a rusted pipe into the roadside ditch. The springwater was safe to drink when Laura lived here, and she remembers people used to fill jugs from the pipe, but nobody uses the springwater nowadays, and there's more water welling up from the ground below the two-tiered foundations than there is coming out through the pipeline.

When the Dickey family bought up the area, most of the small houses of the mill village were frame or stone, and the Dickeys built more of the same for their workers, creating a prosperous company town. Rows of stone houses in the General Grant style appeared, alongside more whitewashed clapboard houses. In 1885, the cornerstone of the Dickey Memorial Presbyterian Church was laid, and this church, with its red tin roof and white-shingled walls and steeple, still has an active congregation today. Frame additions were made to a stone house at 5002 Wetheredsville Road to create a primary school, and as the community continued to grow, a larger public school was built in 1902.

But around the same time, Dickeyville's water-powered mills, with their machinery headed toward obsolescence, began to fall behind swifter, more modern mill systems. The Dickey family lost control of the mill operation in 1909, their three-hundred-acre spread began to be broken up and sold off, and Dickeyville slipped into its own small depression, well ahead of the nationwide financial crash of 1929. The unemployment caused by the mill failure set residents adrift, and Dickeyville had enough buildings vacant to take on the aspect of a ghost town. In 1934, the heart of the Great Depression, the whole town—sixty acres and eighty-one houses, plus the mill complex—was sold to a holding company at auction for $42,000.

At that point, Dickeyville began a carefully planned recovery. The remaining residents consciously set about making their village attractively quaint. A rule that all

buildings must be painted white was laid down by the
Dickeyville Improvement Association, founded in 1937,
and restorations and new construction (supervised by the
architect Howard A. Stilwell) were undertaken in a pre-
scient spirit of historical preservation, though Dickeyville didn't go on the National Register of Historic
Places until 1972. Thanks to this careful planning, the
Dickeyville of the twenty-first century is very meticu-
lously preserved indeed. Most buildings have stayed on
their small nineteenth-century footprints. Additions and
renovations are unobtrusive to the point of being invisible, at least from the outside. The backyards we're passing
are thoughtfully landscaped, without seeming mani-
cured—there's a certain wild feel to the decorative trees
and shrubs and rushes that have been planted here. There
are a couple of arched-wire trellises and plenty of white
picket fences, one of them enclosing a tiny swimming
pool, now covered with canvas for the winter. Within
one of these fences, a dear little wood-frame playhouse
has its *own* white-railed porch, echoing the full-sized
Dickeyville houses so faithfully that I am moved to wonder
whether perhaps there is a dollhouse inside the playhouse
that . . . and so on into infinite recession.

We're walking in back of a brick-trimmed, rubblestone barn of a building, erected as a warehouse for the
mill and converted by Lawrence Sangston in the 1930s as
a live-in studio for the painter R. McGill Mackall. A fair
number of Dickeyville structures are built of these odd

chunks of brown stone, mortared together into a smooth front. Rosebushes twine along what used to be Mackall's back fence. Next door, a canvas hammock twists in the wind, to the tune of water rushing smoothly over a dam in the Gwynn's Falls. The exuberant, muscular bronze nude, arching her whole torso to the sky as she kicks out her muscular right leg, is presumably not Mackall's work, though he probably would have liked it.

Born and raised in Baltimore, Mackall trained in various European art schools, including the Académie Colarossi in Paris, and after serving in World War I he returned to Baltimore to direct the Maryland Institute College of Art. He kept up a busy career painting portraits, murals, stained glass, and scenes from local history—notably, the sewing of stars and stripes on the flag that flew over Fort McHenry during the bombardment commemorated in Francis Scott Key's national anthem. The fort's commander commissioned a widow, Mrs. Pickersgill, to sew the flag, whose dimensions were so large that the seamstress and her thirteen-year-old daughter had to repair to Claggett's Brewery, nearby, to finish the job. This scene, as rendered by "Gillie" Mackall, now hangs in the Carling Brewery plant off Exit 9 of the Baltimore Beltway, and the flag itself is in the Smithsonian Institution in Washington.

By the late sixties, Mackall had evolved into a cranky old man who chased kids, snarling, if they crossed his backyard. In those days, too, Laura remembers seeing, once when her father took her to work with him, a vast mural of nineteenth-century Baltimore life painted by Mackall for the lobby of the *Sun*. In the 1980s, when Laura was a young *Sun* reporter herself, the mural began to be seen as an embarrassment because it portrayed black people in subservient roles, and it was covered over, though not, she thinks, destroyed.

By the time Laura moved here with her family in the sixties, the westward expansion of Baltimore City had rolled right over Dickeyville, but thanks to its sharp natural boundaries, the town is easier to swallow than to digest. Tucked into the cleft of the Gwynn's Falls streambed, it managed to remain, outwardly at least, a nineteenth-century mill town completely unaffected by the twentieth-century city that parted and rejoined around it on the flatland above. During Laura's childhood, the stream was a magnet for the black kids of Forest Park, and she and the other white Dickeyville kids chased crawdaddies around the rocks with them, mixing easily enough in those otherwise uneasy days of the late sixties (though I have the impression their parents didn't socialize across the color line).

In April of 1968, the assassination of Martin Luther King touched off rioting all over the United States, and for once Baltimore was no exception. Riots and looting went on for three days, and much of the inner city was burned. Governor Spiro Agnew had begun his term with a good understanding with Maryland's black leadership, but that had already begun to erode during disturbances elsewhere in the state in 1967. In 1968, the chaos on the streets quickly proved unmanageable for the city police, and Agnew summoned first the National Guard, and then a force of paratroopers from the Eighteenth Airborne Corps—for a total of five thousand troops in town by the time order was restored on April 10. West Baltimore was a major hot spot during the '68 riot, and the damage there took a long time to repair, but the unrest made just a faint impression on a ten-year-old living in Dickeyville, which is testimony to just how thoroughly detached from its actual time and place this small community can be. Laura remembers that the assassination of King frightened her more than the assassination of Robert F. Kennedy (which makes a lot of sense if you think about it), but (although in fact they weren't) "the riots seemed very far away."

Baltimore dodged the busing bullet for longer than many cities, thanks to a rule that students could choose any school in the city to attend so long as they managed to get themselves there and back every day. In Laura's time, the white kids of Dickeyville went to primary school with the black kids of the adjacent neighborhoods at Dickey Hill Elementary, a gloomy brown cube still standing east of Windsor Hill Road. For junior high, grades seven through nine, the white kids went to Rock Glynn and the black kids went to Lamell. They found each other again, sort of, at Western High School later on, but after three years of separation they had lost their ease with one another.

By the mid-seventies, the courts had discerned that the transportation catch in Baltimore's open schools policy (though more fair and less complicated than what existed in many other cities) resulted in de facto segregation far more often than not. As a command solution began to appear inevitable, Western High School, with its magnetic "A-course" college-prep program, came under pressure from more and more students, many from the Catholic middle schools, looking for refuge in an educational environment that suddenly offered far less options than before. Laura did a year of the A course at Western, then switched to Wilde Lake High School in Columbia, a planned community west of Baltimore that had, in those days, a certain utopian vision of itself.

After high school, she went to Northwestern University, because she liked Chicago and was attracted by the Medill School of Journalism at Northwestern. Not so attractive was Medill's proposition that students stick around (and pay the tuition) for a fifth year in order to get job-placement help. Laura reacted by applying to some fifty newspapers all over the United States, and landed her first job at the *Waco Herald-Tribune*. From there, she moved to a six-year stint at the *San Antonio Light*. In 1989, she came home to the *Baltimore Sun*. When she left the paper twelve years later, she had published more than four thousand pieces in her career as a working journalist, not to mention her first half-dozen mystery novels. Since she left the *Sun* in 2001, she has published two "non-series" novels (*Every Secret Thing* and *To the Power of Three*), which, while they are still mysteries in their way, have put her on the road to becoming the sort of social realist that Elmore Leonard became.

We find our way between the L-shaped remains of a stone foundation and the concrete spillway beside the dam. There's a small pond here, with a smooth sheet of concrete spilling quietly over the southern end of it. Above the stilled water, a red metal sign is tacked to a tree:

DANGER!
POLLUTED WATER
KEEP OUT

BALTIMORE CITY HEALTH DEPARTMENT

. . . flanked by the appropriate seals and signets. I wonder, silently, if kids in today's Dickeyville pay any more attention to that than Laura did in her time.

Since it's a Sunday of a holiday weekend, the yellow dozers and diggers on the bridge where Forest Park Drive crosses the Gwynn's Falls are quiet still, but because of the construction the footpath under the bridge has been closed off with a lot of garish orange plastic netting. Though it looks like a few people have made their way through this barrier, we decide to take a detour, cutting between the houses and climbing back up to Pickwick Road, toward a huge old plane tree that grows behind a retaining wall on the steep slope on the far side of the street. The ancient bricks of the sidewalk here are all catty-cornered, thanks to the rippling of roots underneath. Mackall's loading door, mostly overgrown by wisteria, faces the Odd Fellows Hall across Pickwick—another rubblestone building, picked out with bloodred shutters. A few doors down is a tight row of stone houses (one whitewashed and the other not) thought to have been built by George Ware in 1874.

But we are headed the other way, toward Forest Park Drive, which was a boundary for Laura when she was a child. She was abjured not to cross it, and that was a rule she respected. Then and now, this road carries a lot of fast traffic from a world outside the time capsule of Dickeyville—from Forest Park west past the stub of I-70 to the Baltimore National Pike and the 695 I-beltway. Those neighborhoods aren't exactly *bad* even now, but in the seventies they began to slip a little, and Dickeyville residents were advised to carry a little mugger money if they went on a very long walk, though Laura never had to use hers. Her parents sold their house in 1984, as many in the neighborhood began to sell out, prompted in part by rising crime rates along their borders.

In the mid-eighties, Dickeyville went into another mild slump, but now, when real estate all over Baltimore has gone sky high, the neighborhood is enjoying a second renascence. A second generation of *Sun* reporters has begun to move in here. Laura and David Simon have been thinking about a second home, and they were looking at houses in New Orleans right before Hurricane Katrina hit, but all along she had it in mind that a getaway cottage in Dickeyville might make some kind of sense. It is an effective getaway, too, and a whole lot more convenient than most. The next nearest place with this kind of feel would be somewhere in West Virginia.

Today, we cross Forest Park Drive without incident— no traffic to speak of on Sunday morning, and anyway the bridge is closed—and stroll across Upper Pickwick, a quiet block of pleasant small houses, with their backyards sloping down to the stream. The one on the corner across from the stream is a rubblestone structure that goes back to 1790. Across the way is a far more modest house of whitewashed clapboard, but with a big stone chimney built in the days when people knew how to build a chimney that will *draw.* We circle the dead end and go back toward Dickeyville's center on Pickwick proper, the original Pickwick, passing the Presbyterian church and Ashland Chapel—the white Doric portico of the latter shaded by the spreading branches of a fir tree. First constructed as a Quaker meetinghouse on land donated by the Wethered family in 1849, Ashland Chapel later became a Methodist church; today, it is a private residence, and it looks like a nice one, too.

And now we're walking up a street called New Pickwick, a street of little white houses built to look more or less like the old ones, though of newer and evidently lighter materials.

New Pickwick tees off onto the stretch of Sekots Road that used to be Laura's sledding hill, a long, fast swoop of concrete curving down the hill to our left. The sled run used to be even longer and higher, till the upper part was closed by trees planted on the slope above the road to screen a housing complex, Windsor Forest Apartments, built there in the late sixties—to the resentment of all the Dickeyville kids. But what's left looks like you could still break your neck on it, given a sled and a hard pack of snow.

Back in the day, a good snowstorm would seal Dickeyville off still more perfectly from the outside world. There was no way on earth that 1960s rear-wheel-drive vehicles could make it out of the Gwynn's Falls gulch. On snow days, Laura's father would have to mush to the top of the hill on foot and catch a bus to the *Sun* in Forest Park. Though Dickeyville is remarkably well sheltered from wind, hurricane season can still provide interest. One near-miss storm flooded most of the houses here, as the level of the Gwynn's Falls rose high and fast.

At the bottom of the sled run (at the point where a speeding sled would wipe out), we leave the road, and start climbing a path through the maples and oak trees, up a spine of woods between Tucker Lane and Wetheredsville

Road. The maple leaves make a brown-carpet rustling underfoot, while the stubborn oak leaves still cling withered to their branches. Roofs and white walls of the houses on the far side of the ridge show through the damp gray boles of the trees, and in the not-so-far-off distance I can hear the sound of falling water. That's the Gwynn's Falls again, but the spring is also somewhere ahead and below us.

There's a numinous quality to a spring—the silent constant welling of water up from the ground. All cultures find them valuable, for all the obvious reasons, and many make them sacred sites—this spring might well have been holy ground to the Algonquins who traded here with Richard Gwynn three centuries back, and what would the Indians have thought when white men harnessed the water to their mills? For a second, up here alone in this lean stretch of woods, I'm feeling a bigger, boomier time warp than the *Brigadoon* quality Laura finds in Dickeyville. People have been walking this watershed for a mighty long time, way long before the first of Dickeyville's homesteaders found their way across the Atlantic Ocean.

Laura casts about for a minute, her white-blond hair blowing back as she turns her head. There ought to be a trail here somewhere, a shortcut she used to take home from sledding, and once she settles on the route she steps out quickly. Laura is the best-looking woman I know who I think could probably punch me out, and she moves with a sometimes-surprising physical confidence. I can keep up with her on the climb, but on the descent I have to slow down—way down—to preserve my blown-out knees, and I watch the blue and white patch of her windbreaker slipping away from me through the trees.

Fells Point

O N A SUNDAY AFTERNOON IN MID–DECEMBER, I drive down to Fells Point and, after circling and searching for ten minutes or so, find somewhere to park my car on Thames Street, which is named, most likely, in honor of the London waterfront. In 1730, a Quaker ship's carpenter named William Fell bought this swampy promontory southeast of the Inner Harbor and the barely chartered Baltimore Town. His son Edward laid out the streets in 1763. Here the river was deep enough to accommodate deep-draft eighteenth-century ocean-going vessels, which the Fell family knew how to refit and refurbish. North of the waterfront a warren of taverns and short-term boardinghouses soon sprang up, featuring all the diversions enjoyed by sailors on shore leave.

In 1793, a French fleet hove into Fells Point, crammed to the gunwales with colonists escaping a slave revolution in Saint-Domingue (today's Haiti). Among them was another ship's carpenter, Joseph Despeaux, and a parcel of nonrevolutionary shipbuilding slaves. Despeaux started a shipyard in Fells Point and set about building a style of swift merchant ship that would soon become known as the Baltimore clipper, whose design had recently been perfected by shipwrights in Baltimore Town and on the Maryland Eastern Shore. In 1797, the first *Constellation* (so named for the new configuration of stars on the American flag) was built in the Fells Point shipyard.

It's been a long time since Fells Point was a busy international port, but for two centuries plus the neighborhood has held on to that raffish atmosphere. Today, Thames Street is lined with bars, though they're none too busy at two o'clock on a Sunday afternoon. Most seem to have just recently opened their doors, to evacuate the funk of last night's spilled beer into the salt air of the harbor. It's the first nice day in a week of very wintry weather. The temperature's climbed to the high thirties, and grizzled old denizens of the neighborhood have come out to catch the pale sun on the steps, their old tattoos a faded background to the glittering piercings and bright body art of the young folk who frequent the Daily Grind coffee shop.

I reach the corner where Broadway runs into Brown's Wharf, a long dock thrusting into the harbor, and head the other way, taking a diagonal across the wide brick plaza in the middle of the street. A couple of gulls fly up at my approach. On my right is Jimmy's, Fells Point's iconic greasy spoon. On my left is the Admiral Fell Inn. The name is a gruesome pun and that's all; there never was any "Admiral Fell," but it's a nice hotel. On the next corner north is Bertha's, another fixture of the neighborhood for many a day, a bar-restaurant with many small wood-paneled rooms that offers seafood of all descriptions, specializing in mussels, and on Sunday afternoons high tea with the possibility of an authentic Scotch egg. There's live music in the tiny saloon on weekend nights, where behind the counter is a wall's worth of the talismanic green and white Bertha's bumper stickers—EAT BERTHA'S MUSSELS—but rearranged by twisted minds and crooked scissors to make new phrases: EAT BARBARA'S BUSH; BUTT MUSCLE ATTITUDE; YO MAMA'S GRITS; FREE CLINTON'S WILLY; EAT LUCILLE'S BALL.

Glenn Moomau has lived upstairs from Bertha's for fifteen years—or no; in actual fact, he lives upstairs in the building next door—but he uses the restaurant as dining room and cocktail lounge and his band, the Blue Flames, plays in the saloon most Friday and Saturday nights. Glenn doesn't have a doorbell, and I don't have a cell phone, so he's suggested that I just go into the street-level store Flashback and ask Robbie to call up for him. It's not that I think this approach is too complicated, but I borrowed a cell phone from my wife.

A minute or so after I make the call, Glenn comes out of the passway between his house and the next one to it, wearing a black cloth coat and headgear that looks like a cross between a flat cap and a beret. We walk east on Lancaster Street and then cut up through the alleys toward Eastern Avenue. In an alleyway, I stop to check out an odd windfall on the pavement: beads, a gold chain, a gold-topped pen, a lipstick case arranged in a pattern on top of a black knit watch cap. Nothing falls like that by accident—somebody seems to have put it there, and I wonder if maybe somebody is planning to come back and get it later, but it also reminds me of a *krazé*. If you see an assemblage like this on a Haitian crossroads, it's a charm, often a malevolent one, whose power is released by being run over and crushed by passing vehicles, and you're better off not touching it, so I don't touch this one.

At the top of the alley, the afternoon light throws a gilt pie wedge onto the brick front of the building across the street: a handsome little row house about the same size as the one Glenn has lived in for fifteen years—renting until recently, when, he tells me as we stride eastward along Eastern Avenue, he bought the place. In all the years he rented, Glenn got to know his landlady, who lived in a house in Bolton Hill and owned another in Mount Vernon, well enough that she appointed him executor of her estate. Thus Glenn found himself a leading player in the closing acts of a family soap opera, for better or worse—but one of the better results is that he now owns his home . . . and is himself the landlord for the three other apartments and the three stores in the building (Kasbah Café and Own Guru Records along with the Flashback enterprise, which was founded by Edie the Egg Lady and purveys "fun stuff," including but not limited to secondhand CDs, records, videos, and porn). It's a proposition that really can't lose—for although Fells Point still retains its old aura of international souk, its housing stock has climbed to a level that few but yuppie stockbrokers can afford.

Eastern Avenue is the northern border of the neighborhood (though there's also an Upper Fells Point, not much different, to the north), an arterial street that runs all the way out into Essex and Middle River. We pass Tochterman Tackle, open since 1916 at this address, with a quarter acre of fine fishing poles inside, waving gently like reeds in the wind. The way-cool sign, featuring a bass angrily breaking water with a Tochterman lure hooked in its mouth, has been there since 1938. On the approach to Chubbie's Club at the corner of Eastern and South Washington Street, Glenn tells me that this joint used to be the last stop before utter and complete retirement (or equivalent) for knocked-about aging strippers.

"You used to see amazing things there . . . ," he says thoughtfully.

"The egg trick?" I inquire.

"Yeah," says Glenn, "and people taking their teeth out . . ."

Chubbie's is closed this afternoon, luckily, perhaps, for all. It is a rather dignified building for the enterprise it houses: a classic little Federal house, bedecked with

five-pointed preservation stars, and carefully and taste-
fully painted in several shades of gray. Across the street is a
funeral home, which I silently suppose may be the next
and ultimate destination of Chubbie's entertainment
alumnae.

We walk on past. The next few blocks of Eastern
Avenue have been taken over by the relatively new but
rapidly growing Hispanic population. When I moved to
Baltimore in the mid-1980s there seemed to be no Latin
Americans around at all, which struck me as strange,
since I was used to Spanish on the street in most of the
neighborhoods where I lived and hung out in New York.
Now, Mexicans and Central Americans have moved in
big time, taking over a tremendous amount of construction and landscaping work, and the next few blocks are
peppered with their *carnicerias* and with Latin restaurants
(or a combination of the two under the same roof, as in
the case of La Guadalupana Restaurante y Tienda), some
of them very good and all of them inexpensive. The Fells
Point area is a great venue for summer festivals, and
Glenn thinks that from the point of view of food and
music and a general good time, the Latino Fest has
become the best of them all.

Eastern Avenue is an arrow into the heart of Baltimore's old immigrant neighborhoods to the east, which
are southern and eastern European, and these blocks were
once dominated by Ukrainians and Lithuanians and Poles.
On the whitewashed brick building on the next corner is a

beige sign announcing the presence of Zwaig & Zwaig: Abogados—I wonder if it could be an eastern European law firm that's adapting itself to the Spanish trade. Further research reveals, however, that these two attorneys are Argentinian.

How are the new immigrants from Mexico, Central America, and South America assimilating with the old immigrant communities, from Greece and Poland and Italy and Russia? I get a clue by stopping into a High-landtown bar one afternoon, where the barmaid, a classic model with a ratty green housecoat, cat-eye glasses, and a Hon beehive of lurid orange hair, every strand of it brittle with lacquer—

THAT'S A NEW FLOOR! she bellows to a couple of customers toward the back of the joint. ITSA MES-SACANS! THEY SPIT ON THE FLOOR!

Keep them out then, a customer suggests.

I CAN'T DO THAT! THEY SPEND TOO MUCH MONEY! THEY COME IN HERE ON A FRIDAY NIGHT AND SPEND A LOT OF MONEY!

No more than what he spends himself, the customer supposes. I'm here every other day, he claims, but the barmaid snorts and bellows louder, I AINT SEEN YOU IN A MONTH. DON'T TELL ME WHAT THEM MESSCANS SPEND. EVERY FRIDAY NIGHT I'M IN HERE AND I KNOW WHAT THEY SPEND.

Throughout, a Latin-looking gentleman at the far end of the bar is working his way slowly down a bottle of

Bud Ice, then eventually ordering another, which he is courteously served. So I figure the new ethnic influx will blend in comfortably enough in the long run.

At the next corner, we cut up into Patterson Park, and walk on a northeast diagonal, skirting the lower edge of an artificial lake. The surface is a little scummy today, and a couple of cartons and cans are floating—not too many. At the far end a wooden boardwalk runs through a stand of reeds. To our right, on the south side of Eastern Avenue, appear the gilded onion domes of Saint Michael the Archangel Ukrainian Catholic Church, a sort of Disneyland fantasy structure completed in 1991, roughly a hundred years after the first western Ukrainians began to flow into this neighborhood. The first congregants held services in the homes, and later at a smaller version of Saint Michael's on South Wolf Street, till the growth of the parish required a larger and distinctly more colorful building.

The park gets its name from William Patterson, an early Baltimore merchant prince who put his fortune on the line to buy French munitions for George Washington's army—it was his youngest daughter, Betsy, who married Napoléon's brother Jérôme. Patterson donated six acres to found the park in 1827, and in 1850 the city bought twenty-nine more acres from his heirs. Since then, it's been one of the most popular parks in Baltimore. But there're only a few people here, this December day. The branches of the shade trees are stripped and gray, saving as always a few stubborn oak leaves, or here and there a shred of windblown plastic. Just past the lake a guy has stopped astride his bike to feed something out his shoulder bag to an assemblage of at least thirty grounded seagulls. Stark white against the yellowing winter grass, the gulls are weirdly quiet and motionless, their beaks all turned to the bicyclist's bread-bag, waiting placidly for their crumbs, like a herd of cows in a field.

We're walking briskly, since it's still pretty cold, and approaching the north side of Patterson Park. Across Baltimore Street appears the gray stone pile of Saint Elizabeth's of Hungary Roman Catholic Church, flying a banner for the Patterson Park Public Charter School that reads, "Open September 2005—*Hablamos Espanol*—Now enrolling pre-K through 4th grade," on the 1895 rectory to its east. It's a response, however tentative, to the catastrophe of the Baltimore City public school system—neck and neck with the schools of Washington, D.C., for worst in the nation. In Baltimore, the last of the middle class bailed out of the public schools in the early nineties. As our own daughter approached school age, we saw our most committed-to-public-education friends give up and pull their kids out of the last couple of northside schools that had seemed viable. Ten or fifteen years before that, when a rule came out that all public school students must carry their gear in *a mesh bag or other transparent container* produced a brief vogue for Lucite-looking backpacks, I had already begun to suspect that the Balti-more schools had lost the ground they were supposed to be standing on. There is a good, and very expensive, set of private schools here, and the parochial school system is healthy, but charter schools in neighborhoods like Patter-son Park might help narrow the widening educational gap between haves and have-nots in this town, and they may also begin to restore some of the local involvement in and accountability of schools that the federalization of the public system pretty well destroyed. A lot of public money gets thrown at the school problem, both here and in D.C., but you don't seem to see a whole lot of positive results, and Glenn figures that much of the money goes up in graft.

Glenn worked at the *Washington Post* for two years in the late eighties, and before the Pell Grant program was shut down he taught English and writing classes at the Maryland House of Correction in Jessup, a maximum-security prison known on the street as the Cut (which receives a fair proportion of Baltimore inner-city-school alumni and dropouts); he now teaches English at Ameri-can University in D.C., and he got interested in charter schools in D.C. through sending AU students to one to do reporting and, eventually, service learning. He volun-teered at the SEED Public Charter School, which boards its students to better protect them from the temptations and risks of the street. Any student can enroll, no matter how underachieving, but all students must get their grades up to a certain level and sustain it, or they can't stay. The results have been satisfying—every member of the SEED school's first graduating class was admitted to at least one college.

We hit the northeast corner of the park and turn south on Linwood Avenue—Glenn thinks it might be nice to live in one of the very small and modest row houses across the street from the park—to catch the expansive sunset view. It's just a little early for sunset right now, but the slanting afternoon light is shifting the color and mood of the bleached grass and bare trees of the park. So we stop for a moment and look west. This block of Linwood is up on a rise and we have a panoramic view across the grassy swells of the park. Westward on another eminence called Hampstead Hill, the 360-degree balconies and pagoda roof of the Patterson Park Observatory sprouts out of the feathery gray upper branches of the surrounding trees. This building, which everyone now calls simply the Pagoda, was designed by architect Charles H. Latrobe (the son of Benjamin Henry Latrobe, who created many other Baltimore monuments) and built in 1891 on a site called Rodgers' Bastion.

During the War of 1812, that hill was fortified for defense against the invading British, in a somewhat atypical burst of interracial cooperation: "You'll see a master and slave digging side by side," wrote a young Baltimore belle observing these scenes. "There is no distinction whatsoever." Flush with having just burned down most of

Washington, British troops did appear here in September 1814, but they had already failed in their naval assault on Fort McHenry, and the hundred cannon and twenty thousand troops in the Hampstead Hill fort disheartened them. Some say they were also discouraged by the famously crushing late-summer heat. Whatever their motives, they returned to their ships and sailed away.

Some fifty years later, Union troops took over this hill, along with several others around town, to secure themselves against Baltimore's numerous and sometimes violent Confederate sympathizers. After the Battle of Gettysburg, Hampstead Hill became a hospital for some of the thousands of Union soldiers wounded there. Of very mixed sentiments during the Civil War, Baltimore got its long-lasting "Mobtown" sobriquet in 1861when a troop of Massachusetts volunteers was attacked on Pratt Street by rioting pro-Southern civilians; in this episode, reportedly, the first blood of that amazingly destructive conflict was shed. Today's Baltimore struggles on different fronts, no more and no less clearly drawn. Beyond the Pagoda, on the northwest edge of Patterson Park, the Butcher's Hill neighborhood (celebrated by Laura Lippman and thoroughly investigated by her heroine Tess Monaghan in the novel named for that neighborhood) has come back since the 1970s from a spell of decline that began during World War II, and thanks to its century-wide spectrum of architecture, the neighborhood has been on the National Register of Historic Places since the 1980s. But the rest of Patterson Park Avenue, along with the neighborhoods west of it, remains pretty dicey. I have a friend who mentors a kid from this neighborhood through a Big Brother program, and after years of one-step-forward-two-steps-back, he arranged for the boy to go to an out-of-town boarding school with a similar mission to rescue jeopardized children as the charter school Glenn works with in D.C.

Beyond Butcher's Hill on the northwest diagonal, we can see a couple of sky-high cranes around Johns Hopkins Hospital—embattled for decades by surrounding slums, to the point that in the late eighties doctors routinely got carjacked right out of the hospital garage. Since those bad old days, the hospital complex has been widening its perimeter (creating a Baghdad-style Green Zone, Glenn and I joke) by razing tenements, draining the swamp. Doubtless something will be built on all of this suddenly empty space, but just emptying it could create, from one point of view at least, a more salubrious atmosphere for patients and health-care workers alike.

Sunny or not, it gets kind of cold if you just stand there, so we start walking south this time, crossing the path of a nice-looking-strong-looking blond young woman I'll call Alya, who's wheeling her sleeping infant home from her job as afternoon bartender in one or another Fells Point watering hole. Glenn knows her a little, well enough to ask her if a lot of Ukrainians are still coming into the neighborhood these days. Alya, releasing the red rubber stroller handles to cock her hands on her denim hips, reminds Glenn that in fact she's Lithuanian, anyway; as for immigration from that general area of the globe, she shrugs, and says in a still-heavy accent, "They come legal, stay illegal." Which one might call the American way!

Alya does in fact live in one of those sunset-blessed row houses on the east side of Linwood, and she's eager to get her baby inside before he wakes up, and none too eager to talk to inquisitive strangers about immigration issues, so we go on our way. Once we've heard her storm door bang behind us, Glenn thinks out loud that Alya came some years ago on a student visa, and she might have got married, and she certainly seems to have had a child and . . . well, he also thinks I ought to go some time to one of the community suppers at the Lithuanian Hall, especially to check out some kind of honeyed liquor they make, and I feel like maybe I have heard of this stuff, and maybe it is called, in the Georgian rather than Lithuanian context, *boilo,* and maybe they used to make it by percolating bourbon through a basket of fruit instead of coffee, and by now we have come back to Eastern Avenue and are headed farther east into Highlandtown, and certainly by now I have forgotten Alya's real name together with all particulars of her immigration situation: quite likely she wasn't a Lithuanian at all, but a Czech, and maybe she wasn't a woman but a transvestite, and probably she didn't have any baby and stroller but was walking a bat-eared

French bulldog on a thread-thin silver leash. Or was it a spider monkey on her shoulder? I don't know.

Most other Baltimore neighborhoods sacrifice a few squares of pavement per block to trees, but not Highlandtown. Trees attract birds, Glenn explains, and birds crap on cars. People in Highlandtown cut down trees, and the smooth expanses of their sidewalks are uninterrupted by guano, or shade.

On the first corner east of the park is the Patterson Theater, sporting the last vertical marquee left in Baltimore, a small Art Deco treasure. The theater opened in 1930, when Highlandtown was a bustling working-class neighborhood, and stayed open until 1995. In 2003, it opened again as the new headquarters of Baltimore's Creative Alliance—itself a peripatetic institution born in Fells Point, and later housed in a vast, rambling, crumbling Highlandtown Moose lodge (then undergoing a leisurely process of renovation by one of Glenn's buddies, artist Dan Schiavone), and then in a former Pep Boys auto parts store just a few blocks from here, on South Conkling Street, and finally, permanently the Patterson, which has among its assets two galleries, performance space, and several nicely appointed studio apartments on the second floor for the use of artists in residence. The Creative Alliance is a hive and haven for every artistic activity imaginable—the senior Alonsos taught tango here, to pick a typical example, until they got their own space at Gardel's.

One of the first crop of artists in residence, poet and novelist Christine Stewart, is a friend of mine, so I rattle the Patterson's doors, but they don't seem to be open on Sundays, and I forgot to arm myself with her phone number, and finally it occurs to me that she's in California this weekend anyway. Glenn and I go on our way across Eastern Avenue, passing Matthew's, the oldest pizzeria still running in Baltimore, which serves among other things an excellent homemade Italian sausage and is well worth a visit for its bathroom doors alone: his'n'hers featuring, respectively, life-sized hand-painted replications of Michelango's *David* (strategically draped in a loincloth, since this is a family restaurant after all) and Botticelli's ineffable Venus on her half shell. We pass the sundries shop where I got the red fuzzy letters of 𝕰̂𝖙𝖗𝖊 𝕳𝖚𝖒𝖆𝖎𝖓 ironed on to the back of my denim jacket, and a bridal store, Stella's, about half a block long. In the window of the Coral Reef aquarium store, a big plaster shark surges up over the shoulder of a placid Saint Francis and a trio of demurely pious plaster angels; inside, there are maybe a hundred small tanks of exotic fish, festooned with the warning DON'T TAP THE GLASS.

We pause at the corner of South Clinton Street to brood over the demise of Haussner's, which was owned by the same family for seventy-three years before it finally closed in 1999, after much public protestation that it would never close. A fixture of old Baltimore, Haussner's served a blend of German and classic Maryland cuisine, and was renowned not only for its desserts but for its extraordinary collection of nineteenth-century paintings, which sold, after the restaurant's closure, for more than $12 million. Today, the big creamy corner building is occupied by Dunstin's, a laboratory restaurant for Baltimore International College (a culinary school), but ten months on Dunstin's will be closed, and the Haussner's building again for sale.

Here's the Value Village thrift shop where Glenn used to buy most of his clothing, and a couple of pawnshops where he used to find nice obscure little guitar amps (which he uses to amplify his harmonicas)—these pawnshops are still open, though the great global flea market of the Internet has killed a lot of them around Baltimore, and all over the country. Here, too, is the City Pet Center, a boarding kennel for dogs, with charming pups sketched in vintage neon above the center's door. In evidence of recent demographic changes, we have also Esthetica Latina Unisex, styling of men and women alike. We pass the world's last operational Little Tavern. These hamburger joints, with their green-tiled pitched roofs and rather incongruous Tudor cottage affect, used to be peppered all over town, and many of the buildings remain, all of them converted to some other use, if not boarded up altogether. The Highlandtown Little Tavern, Glenn assures me, is the last that still serves hamburgers; there's a HELP WANTED sign in the window, but we don't apply.

A hard-core blue-collar neighborhood in its prime, Highlandtown once got full employment from nearby canning plants and the National Bohemian brewery, and from the steel mills and a GM plant (just recently closed and slated for teardown), not much farther off. During the Civil War, the next Union army post east of Hampstead Hill was atop what was then known as Snake Hill. When the war ended and the soldiers left, Irish immigrant Thomas McGuinness sketched out a village. In 1870, residents changed its name to Highlandtown. The village filled up with Irish and Germans in the last decades of the nineteenth century, and then, as Baltimore City spread eastward to embrace it, absorbed a new wave of immigration from Greece and Italy and eastern Europe.

The nineteenth-century Highlandtown housing stock was brick, with the classic white marble stoops. Later on, most of these row houses were faced with Formstone, a particolored cement siding branded by Albert Knight in 1937 and supposed to look like actual masonry if you are very, very good at supposing. It also has some insulation value, so the Baltimore utility companies encouraged it. Formstone spread over most of Baltimore's working-class neighborhoods like wildfire or a skin disease, and is right up there with the beehive hairdo as taste so bad it's . . . sorta good.

Along with Formstone goes the high-kitsch practice of screen painting. The first painted screens served the purpose of one-way glass, blocking the view of passersby while still permitting insiders to see out. Once upon a time, every other window displayed a mesh image of a kitten or a waterfall (in the thirties, there were supposed to be one hundred thousand painted screens in Baltimore—I don't know who counted them), but screens wear out a lot faster than concrete, though you can still find a few here and there. The twenty-first-century real-estate boom has changed the aspect of some of these houses (renovators typically expose the original brick, then jack up the price by a hundred grand) but there's still a lot of Formstone in Highlandtown.

There are also dozens of deliciously inviting little neighborhood bars all over the place, in the converted parlors of the same little row houses their customers live in. I play a very occasional gig around here with a pickup band sometimes called Anything Goes, and a few years ago, when we rolled out of the Pep Boys venue at two in the morning, one of the more energetic Creative Alliance founders, Megan Hamilton, roused the owners of the bar next door and let them know they needed to reopen for our benefit (explaining to us behind her hand that the owners were new to the neighborhood and didn't understand how things worked quite yet). This afternoon Glenn is explaining to me the fundamental necessity for three bars per block, which is to say that in Highland-town's heyday every small room of every tiny house would be packed to the ceiling with irritable wives and screaming children by the end of the day, so that the weary worker, homeward bound, would absolutely require at least a half hour of attitude adjustment before stepping across the footlights of the domestic scene.

LIVE, WORK, DIE was the Highlandtown bumper sticker of that period, and the principle a couple of generations of residents lived by. Then the GM plant closed, and the canneries relocated, and the steel mills slowed to a point below the threshold of human perception, and unemployment gutted the neighborhood, leaving its youth to the usual fallback solutions of drug dealing, addiction, and petty crime. Twenty-first-century Highlandtown, though, has a renaissance happening that looks fairly durable, and in fact the Creative Alliance has played a large part in giving the neighborhood a whole new flavor of attraction. Highlandtown also has its own personal bard in Rafael Alvarez, another *Baltimore Sun* alumnus who writes lovely elegiac stories, both fiction and non-, about the neighborhood and its denizens (*Orlo and Leini, The Fountain of Highlandtown, Storyteller,* and *Hometown Boy*).

We pass a small branch of the public library—closed, like many branches in neighborhoods that could use them most. But next, across South Conkling Street, is a giant hole in the ground where a new and much larger library branch is under construction on the site of another old movie house. From here, Eastern Avenue swoops down the east side of hill, shoots under a couple of railroad trestles, and emerges into Greektown, whose commercial strip includes a tight pack of restaurants, of which the best known is Ikaros, and storefront churches like the Metropolitan Church of God. Shooting on through, Eastern Avenue wraps around the Johns Hopkins Bayview hospital complex, then drives on across the Back River into Essex.

But we turn south on South Conkling Street, pausing next to a fire station for Glenn to pick up a free copy of the *Baltimore Guide* from a rack in front of its office here. The paper has covered South Baltimore neighborhoods since 1927: by Glenn's reckoning, the most interesting part is the police blotter. For example:

> *A woman told police that her 16-year-old niece threatened her with a kitchen knife following a disagreement about her lack of respect for her aunt. The niece was arrested.*

> *Police officers working a plainclothes detail saw three men make racial insults at another man, throw coins at him and tell him to bring back five friends and they would "(mess) you up." The officers arrested the three men.*

> *One man was arrested for pointing a B.B. gun at another.*

> *An officer on routine patrol in Patterson Park saw two males, whom he described as black, with one wearing a red, black and white shirt. He got out of his car and*

was attacked. He told officers he had been struck in the head and shot in the chest, although his bulletproof vest did not allow the bullet to penetrate.

On the corner of Fleet Street stands the immense gray stone Sacred Heart of Jesus church, whose cornerstone is chiseled AD 1908. A stone tablet facing the street lists an "Honor Roll" of the parish's World War II dead, and the names (Angelona . . . Digiovannie . . . Kelly . . . Krueger . . . Pulaski . . . Sojak . . . Sullivan . . . Wittstadt) cover this area's broad ethnic span. There are not quite as many churches as bars around here, but there are a lot (and, of course, they are bigger). Most have big convent buildings standing next to them, but given the sharp and deep decline in vocations of late, most of these are now standing empty, if they haven't been converted to alternative uses, such as charter schools. The posts of Sacred Heart's grand neo-Gothic portal are emblazoned with the warning NO LOITERING ANYTIME.

We walk another block or so and stop to contemplate a glossy magazine rumpled in a drift of leaves; it's landed open on a big black-and-white picture of Rosa Parks, wearing glasses and a toothy smile, her head held high, and sort of hopeful, under a bold black headline: **Gone but Not Forgotten.** Two months, or not quite two months, have passed since she died. It seems to me that the last time she made the news was when she got mugged in her own apartment sometime in the nineties, and there's something sort of discouraging about that. There's something about the way the image lies among the leaves that reminds me of the beads and trinkets draped over the black watch cap in that Fells Point alley, and I wonder if somebody has come back for that stuff by this time, or if it really was a *krazé* after all.

We're in Canton now, on Brewer's Hill. This neighborhood was so dubbed by John O'Donnell when he settled here in the 1780s. A seafarer who made his fortune importing luxuries from the original Canton in China, O'Donnell numbered George Washington among his customers for a time. In those days, Canton was his plantation—three thousand acres worth—and crowds came out from Baltimore for horse races and the beer gardens along the Patapsco's bank and to taste the peach brandy O'Donnell distilled. His son, Columbus, got up a corporation, and by the mid-nineteenth century had turned Canton into the first industrial park in the United States. Conkling Street, where we're standing now, and many of the other streets fanning north from the shoreline, were named after partners in that original Canton company.

The Baltimore & Ohio Railroad, founded around this time as well, ensured that products imported to or made in Canton could find their way to their customers overland. The idea was to link the Baltimore waterfront with the central Ohio Valley, and to exchange goods in both directions along that route. Charles Carroll, who laid the first ceremonial stone for the B&O railroad in 1828, declared that this performance and the signing of the Declaration of Independence some fifty years before were the two most important actions of his entire life. Then the canneries came, and the brewery we're looking at, and immigrants came up the river to put all that food into all those cans; they occupied Canton's row homes and then spread north into Highlandtown.

Factories and canneries replaced the shipyards on the Canton waterfront. In 1873, a pressure cooker invented in Baltimore by Mark Owings Shriver allowed food to be cooked for canning about four times faster than before—in response, a hundred or so new canneries sprang up all around the harbor's edge from Canton south to Locust Point. Many of the workers were women, and they kept canning steadily through the Depression, till World War II redirected the energy, at least somewhat, toward war production.

In the 1960s, the factories of Canton began to go dark, and in 1965, two blocks worth of housing were razed to make way for the projected (never-to-be-built) East–West Expressway. Some three hundred families were displaced, their homes confiscated on the principle of eminent domain, the prices offered them insufficient for them to buy comparable housing elsewhere. When the expressway didn't happen, the flattened area along the Canton waterfront remained a wasteland for about twenty years, till the late 1980s, when developers began to buy.

Now survivors of the sixties' condemnation, typically paid around $5,000 for their confiscated homes, can go down and admire quarter-million-dollar town houses built on the same sites. Around the same time, the empty factories and canneries along Boston Street began to be converted into luxury condos. These buildings can hold a lot of new-minted gentry, and most of the hundreds of apartments stacked over Boston Street have a water view, and many also can offer a slip in the pleasure-boat marinas that have replaced the commercial port. Most of the Formstone is gone from the row houses nearer the water, and the brick underneath has been repointed, and the doorways tricked out with new brass and faux-colonial light fixtures, and the price of all this has shot up to a level that puts what's left of the old immigrant community under siege.

The National Bohemian brewery is a big brown tower with its back to the Canton Industrial Area, a tremendous tract—10,000 acres when the Canton Company was founded—so that the 225 acres bought by the U.S. government for a military R & D facility during World War I was a hardly noticeable subtraction. Fort Holabird closed in 1970, as most of Canton's other smokestacks began to stop smoking. Glenn's not sure just how much beer is actually brewed in this complex nowadays. An annex to the north side of the tower now advertises Canton Self-Storage. Across the street to the south, another building of the brewery complex has morphed into Brewers' Hill Elder Health. Though Natty Boh

remains a popular potation—cost effective and not half
bad (moreover, according to some it is excellent for
killing garden slugs)—the brand was taken over by
Stroh's long ago and is now manufactured at a plant in
Lehigh, Pennsylvania (not far from the miles-long rusty
graveyard of Bethlehem Steel in that region). A part of
the Brewer's Hill plant was occupied by the Brimstone
microbrewery, till Brimstone was bought out by the
Frederick Brewing Company in 1998.

We are thirsty, come to think, and Glenn remembers
Walt's, one of those nice little neighborhood bars a block
or so southwest of here. He knows a girl, a sometime
stripper (emphatically not a member of the superannu-
ated Chubbie's revue), who sometimes works the bar at
Walt's—she's real sweet, but she's not here today, though
it takes me awhile to figure that out since this afternoon's
barmaid is also real sweet, sporting a navel ring in a roll
of pale pudge that winks at us from between the tails of
a loose, diaphanous, mostly unbuttoned top, and her
demeanor also gives the impression that she might be
planning to strip somewhere else later on. Deeply disloyal
to the no longer locally brewed local brew, I drink a
Corona with a wedge of lime forced down the bottle
neck—why I would be hard pressed to explain, since it's
more or less the middle of winter. The only other customers are a couple of elderly gents, watching football on
a TV behind the bar—at the other end, a keno screen
pulses quietly, but no one's playing that right now. Glenn

thinks not all the regulars are elderly and that some of them are looking at us funny. The sweet barmaid seems sort of sad to see us leave after just one beer, and I am old, bald, and ugly enough to take a little comfort in that.

We keep walking westward, circling a redbrick branch of the Enoch Pratt Free Library to enter O'Donnell Square, which features a life-sized statue of sea captain John, holding his hat in his right hand and gesturing expansively with his left, to welcome you to the wonders of Canton. His left hand swings back toward the waterfront, while his gaze is set in the general direction of the rich Ohio Valley. Once one of Baltimore's numerous covered street markets, the square is now a pleasant long rectangle of open space. Thanks to the influx of well-heeled newcomers in the waterfront condos a few blocks south, the square has had a recent makeover, and its old-school neighborhood bars and restaurants have been joined by a couple of more sophisticated restaurants, notably the excellent Helen's Garden, which draws diners not only from the riverside but from all over Baltimore, not only thanks to the cuisine but also to the presence of Luffy, described by Glenn as a "great and sardonic" waitress who migrated here from John Steven in Fells Point. There's Vaccaro's Italian bakery, either new or greatly spiffed up from its previous avatar, cheek by jowl with the garish yellow sign of Canton Discount Liquors, which remains most unapologetically exactly what it has always been. There are two or three Irish-themed pubs

(Looney's Pub, Coburn's Tavern and Grill) and, toward the northeast corner, a TV and Radio Service, in business since the *Electronic Tubes* its sign advertises were in fact state of the art. It's still a family business, Glenn tells me, a son having recently inherited it from his father, and the place used to feature a talking dog who could say words like "Vit-a-mum," but the dog died. The TV shop, like John's Restaurant and Carryout at the opposite corner of the square, has managed to become charmingly retro simply by staying itself, while the Saint Casimir's CMV Post 1764 has turned into Mama's on the Half Shell, with a saucy mermaid undulating around the corners of its dangling signboard.

High, very high on the tower, the Natty Boh dandy's one eye electrically winks down on the scene. Mr. Boh's aspect has changed very little since his beer was first brewed—an Art Deco stylization of a roaring twenties bon vivant, with a huge handlebar mustache and a curlier version of H. L. Mencken's hairstyle—though he seems far more genial than the dyspeptic Sage of Baltimore. Mr. Boh and Captain John have, oh, very different personal styles! Indeed, O'Donnell has resolutely set his back to the newcomer winking high over his shoulder. But I can imagine that they would have understood each other.

A firehouse, Father Kolbe's school, and Saint Casimir's Roman Catholic Church, its doorway flanked by gold-topped towers, fill the entire block west of O'Donnell Square. Saint Casimir's exterior walls are under repair, and we go past it, skirting the scaffoldings, taking a zigzag route in the general direction of Fells Point. Glenn is avoiding Boston Street for some reason, despite the water view, or maybe because of it—that and the traffic and the noise and the overall sense of yuppie invasion. On Hudson Street, we pass the remnants of the National Can factory, now mostly taken over by a Safeway store— in the good old days, National Can put up oysters and crabmeat shipped up from Crisfield and the other fishing towns strung south along Chesapeake Bay. And the American Can Building now seems to house restaurants on the order of Outback Steakhouse, with Struever Bros. Eccles & Rouse advertising office space upstairs . . . and it definitely shelters the Austin Grill, run by Glenn's brother John for the last ten years. At last, we are squeezed out on Boston Street after all, right in front of Captain James Landing, which Glenn admires for its over-the-top architecture: placed on a peculiar wedge of ground between Boston and Aliceanna Streets, the building is got up to resemble a freighter, so convincingly as to be almost alarming. It was even more convincing, Glenn recalls, when the flood from Hurricane Isabel actually put it in the water.

Away to our left there's a glimpse of pleasure boats along the docks, last afternoon sunlight glinting on aluminum masts, and now we have come into Thames Street again. Glenn snorts at a peculiarly precarious rooftop deck, perched like some kind of circus balancing act on the very peak of a house at the eastern end of a row.

Dodgy as they may look from the ground, these things are popular all over the back streets of Fells Point and Canton and Highlandtown, among residents who'll go to any lengths necessary to get their piece of a water view. Those efforts and achievements are always threatened by the prospect of new waterfront high-rises—the old condos, too, risk having their views blocked by new ones.

It's twilight now, cold and breezy, as we walk the cobblestones west, past the cavernous brick barn of the old City Pier. Built in 1914 as a harbormaster's office, the building eventually became the police station set and general headquarters for the TV series *Homicide,* spun out of David Simon's book of the same title. It's been empty since *Homicide* shut down and cleared out, and Glenn has heard of a plan to convert it into a boutique hotel. A couple of tugboats are moored alongside it, and supposedly they are going to stay. They are picturesque aplenty, to be sure, though Glenn observes that their horns blow him out of bed at 4:00 a.m.—perhaps not an asset to a high-priced hotel room.

Over the years, the factory workers from the neighborhoods just inland took to swimming and sunbathing alongside the City Pier. Back when Glenn first moved to Fells Point, the pier housed Baltimore's Department of Adventures in Fun, under the resourceful direction of the Fun Lady, Virginia Baker, famous for the adage "If it ain't decent and it ain't right, stay away from it." The Fun Lady organized shows of vintage cars and an extravaganza of

Elvis impersonators to celebrate the singer's birthday and kid stuff like turtle races and hog-calling contests (I am sorry I missed out on the latter, since hog calling is one of my many now-useless skills) and lots, lots more. Under her aegis, the name of the building morphed into the "Rec Pier" (if you want to hear that as Wreck Pier, feel free). It remained a mecca for Baltimore fun-seekers till *Homicide* took it over in the early nineties.

At the end of the sixties, Glenn has picked up, Fells Point went through a phase somewhat similar to what occurred a bit later in New York City's East Village—a romantically seedy neighborhood with dilapidated housing and cheap rent, it attracted flocks of artists and writers and their bohemian fellow travelers. John Waters, the master chronicler of Baltimore quirks, spent a lot of time here in those days, and many among his entourage (a.k.a. his cast) lived here then, and many scenes from his early films were shot here.

You could see that scene as a cultural treasure or a big rats' nest or a little of both, depending on your point of view. The whole area was slated for demolition in the early seventies (at the same time that so much of the Canton waterfront housing was mowed down)—when the East-West Expressway project would have replaced most of Fells Point with a giant interstate cloverleaf, if not for a local social worker turned activist. Endowed with the size and the obduracy of a fireplug, Barbara Mikulski emerged from the molten core of ethnic East Baltimore;

her family ran a bakery in Highlandtown, where she grew up. In the course of what she once described as "a transportation Wagnerian opera," she discovered a taste and a talent for politics. Baltimore sent her to Congress in 1976, and she has been a U.S. senator since 1994. The East-West Expressway looked at her twice and fell over dead. True, there is still no speedy way to get clean across Baltimore no matter which way you slice it, but the preservation of neighborhoods like Fells Point and Federal Hill is worth it.

Again we're crossing Broadway Square (which old-timers still tend to call "Red Square"), stepping over a vestigial footprint of a masonry gazebo that was ripped out a few years back because skate rats using it for stunts were considered to be a nuisance. A couple of blocks north, the lower Broadway covered market is still standing— neon squiggles of the coffee-shop signs shining through the twilight. Darkness is falling fast, and the T-shirts and keepsakes seem to leap at us from the brightly lit souvenir shop windows along the next block of Thames Street, where the long-evolving personality of Fells Point has been co-opted into the kind of memorabilia you can find anywhere between Toronto and Timbuktu. At the end of the block now stands an utterly character-free brick and glass cube, housing a North Face sportswear haberdashery.

Thames Street ends just short of a last fin of land jutting into the harbor, a small but significant chunk of real estate, where Fred Bailey, the youth that would become Frederick Douglass, lived as a slave in the 1830s, on the now nonexistent Philpot Street. In 1846, eight years after Douglass caught a train for the North and freedom, the houses were torn down and replaced by a chromium plant. Allied Chemical continued to process chromium here into the 1980s, and after that the area became a Superfund cleanup site, and after that it was paved over, and now it is scheduled for development, under the new designation Harbor Point, by Struever Bros. Eccles & Rouse, or the *apostles of evil,* as Glenn likes to call them for a joke. The balconies on the last batch of new condos will surely be blocked by the new ones built here, but since neither one of us has any chips on that table, it is easy for us both to shrug off.

Tonight, there's a nice view across the darkening water, to Federal Hill and, east of the berm, to Locust Point, another colossal industrial park mostly fallen into desuetude these days, though the huge red neon Domino Sugar sign still glows above the horizon. As a matter of fact, it is one of a pair, and I used to admire the mate to it while crossing the East River on the Williamsburg Bridge's then-seldom-used pedestrian walkway to the Brooklyn waterfront neighborhood where I lived in my twenties. The one in Baltimore is bigger, in fact: 650 neon tubes pulling 750 amps an hour, it costs the company $70,000 a year to keep the sign ablaze from darkness till closing time of the waterfront bars, and the sign needs a weekly maintenance visit to keep 90 percent of its tubes firing on any given evening. Locust Point residents declare that the sign "warms your heart," and Highlandtown's indefatigable chronicler Rafael Alvarez tagged it as "the star by which intoxicated boaters navigate out of the harbor." Glenn seems to have a similar fondness for the Baltimore Domino sign, and is a bit fearful that development trends around the harbor may cause it and the building it rides on to be torn down. Somebody's still cooking something over there, though, because there's a plume of slate-blue smoke puffing up behind the jagged rooflines of the old factories, as the last red traces of a mostly invisible sunset fade behind the Domino Sugar neon.

It's cold enough we can see our breath as we go huffing north up Caroline Street, suddenly beginning to be conscious that we have walked quite aways. Caroline was sister of Frederick Calvert, the sixth and the last Lord Baltimore, and the last noble proprietor of Maryland. Aliceanna Street, an east-west artery through the neighborhood, is named for a Quaker midwife married to John Bond, a partner of William Fell in the settlement of the area. We cut across to Broadway again, and find that we have snuck up on Glenn's house from the north side. Glenn unlocks a metal gate that lets us into a narrow passage between two buildings, with a plank walkway for wet weather. Fells Point lies more or less at sea level, and can ship a good deal of water in storm season, like for instance when Hurricane Isabel came through in 2003.

Inside his second-floor apartment, Glenn throws his coat and hat on a couch and pours himself a glass of port. Walking is good for the soul, he says, but for now it feels good to sit down. Glenn's from West Virginia originally, and you can see that mountain stock in his appearance—rangy, rawboned, and dirty-blond, he lopes like a reasonably amiable panther. He's been accused of being a James Dean look-alike, but to my eye he's a lot more real. One can see that his place is a bachelor pad, but though it might not pass the white-glove test, the state of the place betrays some fundamental sense of order. There might be a dish or two in the sink, but there isn't a whole greasy stack of them. Around the small electronic keyboard Glenn uses to practice his singing, cassettes are piled in slightly dusty towers. Among his other musical enterprises, Glenn (whose last name is a good example of the famous two-five chord change) is lead singer for the Blue Flames, and serious enough about it to have taken voice lessons over the last few years, and to log regular practice time. He's a bit of a collector, not to say pack rat (me, I have no right to call anybody else a pack rat). I'm not sure if he uses all the baker's dozen antique broadcast microphones that line his mantelpiece, for example (possibly a few of them don't work). The bathroom has no hair growing on the fixtures (none); on the contrary, it is pristine, white, and bright, adorned with a Bettie Page shower curtain, and a small painting of Haitian women washing clothes in a river, their own garments wet to seductive transparency (disclosure: Glenn obtained this article from me), and a near life-sized black-and-white photo of a lovely long-ago girlfriend, clad only in a contemplative expression and the word *you* crayoned on her forehead. Glenn always wanted to have a screen porch with a tin roof, and so after he bought the building, he built himself one out the back door that lets him onto a fire escape—it is a rooftop contraption, but nowhere as queasily cantilevered as the one we recently passed on Thames Street, and in season Glenn can stretch out there and listen to the rain on the roof.

A little before six o'clock, he roaches his hair back like Johnny Cash used to (I'm not going for the James Dean thing), picks up a couple of the vintage mikes and one of those old off-brand tube amps and a couple of briefcases full of harmonicas, and I follow him out through the evening bustle, across the Thames Street cobblestones to the Cat's Eye Pub, housed in one of Baltimore's oldest buildings; there must have been some sort of alehouse in this location in the days of William Fell, and elders of the neighborhood recall when this site was a gambling and bawdy house, politely designated as a private "pleasure club." Before he turned himself into a singer, Glenn was (and remains) a stellar blues harp player, courted by the best of the local bands, including the locally renowned psychobilly trio, the Glenmont Popes. He toured with the Popes in their original and extremely potent configuration, before the untimely death of their bass player Randy Rawlinson, and wrote a book about the experience called *Ted Nugent Condominium,* which I invite you to read for yourself if you want an explanation of the title.

Since 1991, Glenn has played the Sunday afternoon slot at the Cat's Eye (which uses a relaxed definition of "afternoon") with pianist Steve Kraemer and the Bluesicians. In fact, I first met Glenn one such afternoon when he was taking a break on the Cat's Eye stoop. Megan Hamilton, journalist and cofounder of the Creative Alliance, whom I had the good luck to meet when she turned up in one of my fiction workshops at Goucher College to finish her degree after, oh, a fifteen-year hiatus, introduced us; she was working there as a bartender at the time. Glenn is a powerful fiction writer, among his other gifts, and he was interested in me for that reason, and since I am an amateur blues guitarist the Sunday afternoon Cat's Eye gig interested me. My dream is a band that only rehearses on stage, and this is one.

In those days, Kraemer would open around four o'clock with a solo set; he was burly and choleric, with the personality of Miles Davis on one of his more misanthropic days, and like Miles he played with his back to the audience, on a battered but serviceable upright piano that came with the venue, I believe. Well, the Cat's Eye isn't Alice Tully Hall, it's a waterfront bar whose patrons tend to be at least half drunk and very noisy, so Kraemer's take-it-or-leave-it-and-fuck-you-either-way attitude made a certain amount of sense. He played a barrelhouse style, mostly instrumentals, but every now and then singing one in a battered but serviceable voice that, in competition with a hell of a lot of background noise, quickly took on a gritty hoarseness. For the second set, he was joined by Glenn on harmonica and Phil Cunneff on drums; Kraemer's left hand has the impact of a whole division of artillery, so he never needed to bother with a bass player, though sometimes he'd get one up there just for fun.

The third set always featured guests, to the point of being a big blues jam with maybe a stand-up acoustic bass and one or a couple of electric guitars and a horn or two added into the mix. People would line up to play on Kraemer's third set, but being a friend of Glenn's gave me an unearned advantage. By that time, the Cat's Eye clientele would be seven-eighths drunk and people would be shouting along out of tune and other people, in a space packed tight as a can of anchovies, would be trying to jitterbug and recklessly elbowing out-of-town bikers at the same time, so you could get away with a few musical mistakes . . . or that was my theory until the first time I got up there with Kraemer and he cut me into a thousand and one thin slices that would, with some olive oil, capers, and Parmesan cheese, have made a nice carpaccio. I can't say I didn't ask for it, though, and in fact it was an educational experience; Kraemer cuts such a fine line

that you can read all the notes you should have been playing off the staff he's engraved in your hide, in case you
feel like practicing for another attempt down the road.

All that was a long time ago, and I figure there is a
good chance Kraemer doesn't remember it—it wouldn't
have been very memorable from his point of view. He
himself has lost so much weight since then that I wouldn't
have recognized him if I hadn't spent enough time in the
bar a couple of Sundays back to identify him on the basis
of his musical style. He's lean and wiry nowadays, and
he's grown his hair out and added a long droopy Zap-
paesque mustache, and he looks even less like a rocket
scientist from NASA than he used to, though in fact he is
associate director of the Institute for Astrophysics and
Computational Sciences at NASA's Goddard Space Flight
Center (as well as professor of physics at the Catholic
University of America). Lately, he's been playing guitar
on a lot of these Sunday gigs—he's almost as impressive
on guitar as piano—but tonight he's hooking up an electronic keyboard. That hammered old upright is gone.

Glenn slips behind the bar and pours a straight shot of
Irish to moisten his throat. There's a changing of the
guard on bartenders, and once Gypsy is enrolled on the
register, I ask him to draw me a pint of beer. Thanks to
the time of year, Gypsy's long white hair and beard
are vaguely reminiscent of Santa Claus, but his dress,
demeanor, and tattoos put you more in mind of the Fate's
Assembly motorcycle club, of which he is in fact a former

member. Gypsy's a really nice guy, Glenn told me, in the same way that a lot of girls Glenn knows are really sweet, and Glenn also told me, while we were walking through Patterson Park, a long story about how some unusually feckless JDs stole Gypsy's chopper one time, though when they learned exactly who wanted it back, it was parked in front of Gypsy's house the next day.

Gypsy looks good for a man of his years, and some of them hard ones, though he claims to be feeling off-color this evening, for reasons that may be related to the night before, or so I gather from the chatter around the bar. Kraemer and Glenn are talking food while they set up, or Kraemer is talking and Glenn is listening. I've heard from Glenn that Kraemer is a gourmet chef, and apparently he recently took a sort of cook's tour of France, and has just got through sending a package of crabmeat to a friend in Brittany, where the crabmeat is the only comestible that's just not as good as it is here. That's because they don't have blue crabs in Europe, I suggest; instead, they've got what we call stone crabs, which are perfectly successful at being crabs, I'm sure, but through no fault of their own just not as good eating. This being Maryland, everybody's got his own specially nuanced crab-cake recipe, and Kraemer, whose ideas about food are as precise and exacting as his ideas about music, quickly runs through his. You should stick the cakes in the fridge for twenty minutes or so before you put them in the skillet, he explains, and that way they won't fall apart. That seems like such a good idea I think I might try it. Kraemer gave Glenn a bottle of wine for Christmas, it seems, and before the set starts he recommends the exact temperature at which it should be drunk, and further suggests that the absolutely ideal way to drink it is out of the belly button of a woman you love.

I'm considering this possibility as the set begins and I return to my pint, though, of course, I don't know what kind of wine is in question, and I suspect that's crucial to the formula. But soon the music is beginning to massage my brain. I remember Kraemer playing with a thundering angry energy on the old upright, but tonight his touch is softer, and more melodic I would say. Steve Potter, the Blue Flames bass player, has been playing the Cat's Eye gig for the last five years or so, bringing the lineup to quartet strength, with the drums and harmonica. Kraemer has lightened up some on the left hand, letting the bassist do his work. He sings in a presentable blues snarl—edge enough on it to hold your attention. I don't know if he's taken voice lessons or not. Probably he gives them to himself.

Glenn keeps the harmonica wailing behind the sad lyric of "Reconsider Baby," that good old Lowell Fulson tune, and I forget what else they build on top of that in the first set, but rest assured you won't hear any of that Same Old Blues Crap here—Kraemer's somewhat obsessive intelligence is always on the prowl for unusual material and interesting ways to play it, and the other guys are well able to bring in a few on their own.

When the band takes a break, Gypsy cues up some canned music, which sounds fairly washed out by comparison. Glenn gets his second straight shot of Irish, and for the next fifteen minutes he and Phil, an imposing-sized man with a gleaming shaved head, discuss the travails Phil has endured this weekend while struggling to install a new water heater. This band ain't as young as it used to be, it crosses my mind as they return to the stand, but then again neither am I. They play some Percy Mayfield tunes this second set: "I Got to Leave You Alone" and "The Highway Is Like a Woman." Glenn cups one of his old bullet mikes to the harp and leans into it, wailing, with his whole upper body, just like he was rocking a baby.

It's nowhere as crowded as usual for Kraemer's second set, and when I mention this to Gypsy, he fires up a small black cigar and grunts, "Everybody's shopping." Out of him comes a thread of blue smoke. "Or broke from shopping." True, Christmas is just a week off. Kraemer, through his teeth and with the ultimate purpose, I suspect, of forestalling any dumb-ass requests for "Jingle Bells," announces the one Christmas song they play every set. "Santa's Been Messing with the Kid" is all about a fat guy with long hair and a beard who sneaks in the house and drinks up the whiskey and kicks the children and fools with the women and it goes on from there . . .

Day after Christmas, Santa aint around
All because they come along and run him outa town
Oh Lord, won't you look what Santa done . . .

By now the Cat's Eye would normally be standing room only and not much of that, but tonight I've got enough room at the end of the bar to turn around if I feel like it, though probably not enough to swing a cat. Unfortunately, there's enough room for the crazed-looking kid who just walked in to find a place at the bar to my left. He's got on a camouflage cap and an oversized ultra-ugly heavy metal T-shirt, with heads of rotting corpses screened in lurid orange over black, and the logo PURE EVIL, which I suppose may be the name of a band, and—dammit, I know better than to make eye contact with crazy people.

Reluctantly, I comply with his request for my name. "Like Madison Square Garden," he says brightly. "I'm Kenny." He thinks for a long time. "Like . . . Kenny's Denny."

I'm really hoping that our relationship is going to end there, but apprehensive that it won't. Kenny scores a glass of water off of Gypsy. Water is free at the Cat's Eye, up to a point. By long-established habit, Kraemer drinks nothing else while he's playing. Kenny takes a sip, coughs, then turns around with a tremendous take and registers the band. "I thought that was the jukebox, or the radio." Well, I already knew he was out of it, but . . . the band is no more than three yards from where he's standing and he could even reach out and touch Phil, if he were that much of a fool.

At last and alas, Kenny finally recovers from his shock at finding live musicians in his vicinity and starts telling me the story of his day, which began at 8:30 this morning when he parked his girlfriend's $21,000 Isuzu somewhere on Charles Street and went looking for beer, reasoning that it would be better for him to travel on foot than to spend the night in the city jail.

He's been looking for the car ever since. He came into the Cat's Eye to look for it. I don't think it would help anything to remind him that Charles Street is not only several miles long but also a few miles away from Fells Point. He left his iPod in the car, too, and he can't remember if he locked it. I ask him if he'd started drinking at 8:30 in the morning, thinking it would be a challenge to find beer in downtown Baltimore at that hour of a Sunday, and he tells me, ducking his head with becoming modesty, that in fact he'd hoisted his first one around noon the day before, but he'd taken a nap before commencing his trip into town from some place called Edgemont, so he was good to drive. He's a little worried about how his girlfriend is going to react to the loss of the car, though, and not really looking forward to telling her about it.

It strikes me that he probably won't be drinking any wine out of *her* belly button any time soon. Kenny's got no money, just some kind of token, I don't know for what, that he keeps twiddling in his fingers. He tries more than once to cadge something from Gypsy—a beer, a cigar, a box of matches, anything—until Gypsy finally narrows his eyes a little and says briefly, "I can't do that," at which point the kid has just enough sense to lay off. I am studying the band through a long cone of tunnel vision that especially shuts out Kenny, his T-shirt, the problem of his girlfriend's car. The crowd has picked up a bit in the last few minutes, and if I hadn't switched off my peripheral vision I would be aware of several people dancing in the open area by the other end of the bar. A snake-thin woman, wearing a long-sleeved black jersey that clings to her bones and a string of silver beads almost down to her ankles, dances right into my tunnel, alone. She does a couple of sliding steps and then a spin that brings her nose to nose with me, and she announces in a flat dull voice, "I'm so depressed."

After a beat in which I might have replied if I could have thought of anything to say, she funky-chickens herself away. I decide I might as well let Kenny back into my world after all, and I spend the next ten minutes or so trying to help him reconstruct the pathway that led him away from that 21K Isuzu, but his mind is like a bucket of glass splinters, and you can't put one on top of another. He remembers a CVS pharmacy, somewhere, maybe—and in a flash it comes clear to him that he had made a conscious decision to leave the car unlocked because there was nothing in it to steal anyway (he's forgotten the iPod, it seems). "Maybe that wasn't a good idea," he says now. Serendipitously, Kraemer is singing "Bad Time to Quit Drinking," which Glenn rates as the best of Kraemer's original songs, so I give Kenny a five spot to buy beer, and after vowing his eternal friendship he sorta drifts away from me, thank God.

In Glenn's estimation, the Sunday afternoon Cat's Eye crowd has aged right along with the band. Moreover, the larger Fells Point scene has changed in the last few years. The neighborhood used to haul in packs of college kids on the weekends from the campuses on the north side of town, but lately most of them have been drawn off to Power Plant Live!—a new complex a block or two west of Gardel's, where the kids can get admitted to nine different venues for one cover charge, some of them rumored to be comfortably slack on the issue of underage drinking. For Fells Point residents, the result is mixed—the bars and restaurants may get a little less business, but then there's a lot less screaming, fighting, and public urination during the small hours of the morning.

The band takes a break, and Glenn comes over to my end of the bar and starts explicating the big wall of portraits, some photos, some paintings—these are all Cat's Eye workers or regulars who have died: Jeff Knapp, Kenny Orye, Wayne Smith, Joe Ennd, Nancy Knapp-Sochor, John Collins, Fred O'Leary, Charlie Newton, Rick Serfas, Donna Jean Silverthorn . . . to name only a few. The biggest canvas is a portrait of Janice High (an apt surname in Glenn's opinion), a buxom brunette sort of dissolving into black around her waistline. She used to be a jailhouse buddy of Squeaky Fromme's, according to Glenn, among her other qualities; she died relatively young and rather mysteriously. Those portraits make kind of a spooky background for the band, Glenn sometimes thinks, and now it's time for him to go back up there.

I study the Wall of the Dead awhile longer, then turn my gaze on the living customers. I watch a middle-aged couple dancing—they might be out-of-town tourists, judging by the man's bright orange ball cap, but it doesn't have the Orioles logo, and his partner is dressed upper-middle-class tasteful, in a black sweater set and pearls. The band plays "Having Fun," by Memphis Slim, and "Merry Christmas, Baby," which, as Kraemer announces with weary relief, will be the very last Christmas song they do . . . till next year. Since Kenny faded, the barstool next to mine has been occupied by a tall, silver-headed dude with the preppy good looks of an L.L. Bean model, and garb apparently from the same source. He's rotated toward the bandstand, with his elbows cocked on the bar behind him, and a little too often he chips into the music with a tomcat screech. There's not enough crowd and anarchy for this to pass unnoticed tonight—and Kraemer finally shouts a question to the guy's girlfriend, who looks more than a little like Liza Minnelli in her salad days, "When are you gonna get him fixed?"

The girlfriend is hugely amused by this crack, but the silver-headed guy is not sufficiently discouraged. Phil, who has a pleasant light voice, sings just one song on every date, and he's just got well started on "Whiskey Drinking Woman" when the guy decides to encourage him with another big caterwaul. Phil drums like white lightning, and has a temper that can sometimes flash like that, too. Holding a drumstick like it was a gun, he draws a bead on the guy and tells him to knock it off. There's just a second of pin-drop silence before Phil breaks contact, bashes a cymbal, and snarls at the others, "Let's do Mojo."

And they do. Kraemer has closed shows with this barnstormer here for twenty years or more. A good big crowd will raise the roof, echoing the familiar lines.

> *Got my mojo working*
> *(got my mojo working)*
> *Got my mojo working*
> *(got my mojo working)*
> *Got my mojo working*
> *But it just don't work on you.*

Abashed now, the silver-headed guy says good night to the room most politely as he shows his girlfriend out. Glenn makes him as typical of the new Fells Point breed—rich enough to buy in at the astronomical new prices, hip enough to want to be near the music and the clubs, but also wanting it quiet by ten, so he can get some sleep. "And obviously never been in a bar before," Glenn grumbles as he stashes his amp in some cranny where only he can come back and find it later.

The next band up is loading in as Kraemer's crew is breaking down. Their guitarist, as it happens, is Tom Diventi of Apathy Press, which published *Ted Nugent Condominium,* and tonight he's got a poetry CD he just brought out to give to Glenn. Everybody wishes everybody Merry Christmas, and Glenn and I walk out into the refreshing cold, a block east to John Steven, a good seafood restaurant if you happen to be in the neighborhood. I get the crab cakes, which might not be as good as Kraemer's crab cakes, but good enough for me.

Charles Street

AT THE END OF THE FIRST WEEK OF MAY, MY neighbor Jack Heyrman and I catch a ride downtown with Jack's wife, Joy. It's Sunday morning, around ten o'clock, and the streets are quiet; the few pedestrians we pass are churchgoers in full regalia. As we near the harbor a band of smallish, well-worked-out young women breaks across Lombard Street and scatters north. By their size and condition, we take this crew for gymnasts at first. "They're all really short," says Jack, "and about to be killed."

But Joy is looking up at the skyline where it's interrupted by her favorite high-rise in downtown—arranged in alternate bands of blue stone and glass that reflect the passing white clouds, it looks like a veritable stairway to heaven. This office tower was completed by Boston architects Cabot, Cabot & Forbes in 1986, but somehow I have always had my nose so tight to the bread-crumb trail that I never saw it before Joy pointed it out today. She drops us off at the corner of Charles and Pratt Streets, and as she guns away up town we cross the street diagonally, to the water's edge where the *Constellation* is moored, finishing her days as a museum.

The *Constellation* is the last all-sail warship to be built and launched by the U.S. Navy. Defined as a "sloop of war," she was bigger than the average sloop, and carried more guns. Launched from Virginia's Gosport Navy Yard in 1854, she spent nearly three years with the Mediterranean Squadron, then was dispatched to inter-cept slave ships coming away from the African course and bound for the U.S. slave markets, among which Balti-more had long been important. She had captured three slavers by the time the Civil War broke out at home—the *Constellation* spent the war years convoying merchant ships to protect them from Confederate privateers, or contributing her weight to the blockade of Southern ports. Today, she is the last Civil War ship still afloat. When my daughter was the right age to enjoy it, we toured the *Constellation* several times—the many well-organized exhibits include (but are not limited to) a piece of salt cod from the Civil War era, which fascinated us both enormously.

This morning, there's a big clipper ship moored just behind the *Constellation,* most likely one of the tall ships that re-create the nineteenth-century sail experience for pleasure boaters all up and down the eastern seaboard.

Jack turns his nose into the wind, remembering his child-hood when all this area was working waterfront—a tremendous seafood market along the dockside, and the air redolent with whatever spice the McCormick company was cooking that day, in a building that once stood a block south on Light Street; Jack remembers going to tea tastings there, too.

Now the old dockside has been turned into a wide esplanade of newish brick featuring an artificial waterfall with some metal sculptures installed in its pools. We cross it to enter one of the Harborplace pavilions—great steel and glass barns opened by the Rouse Company in 1980, part of a waterfront restoration project that succeeded mightily in bringing tourists back to Baltimore's downtown. The inside pocket of the harbor is lined on the north and west by two of these two-story buildings, festooned with decks and outdoor cafés, chock-full of fish markets and souvenir shops and restaurants that range from Hooters to the venerable Phillips Seafood. East is the Power Plant entertainment palace and the National Aquarium, a still more astonishing steel and glass ziggurat which climbs from the dolphin pool at the bottom through a couple of stories worth of circling sharks to the tropical rainforest at its pinnacle. All of this complex ties in to convention hotels on the north side of Pratt Street; the Convention Center is just a block west (now stuffed to the gills with hundreds of frenetic cheerleaders) and the Camden Yards baseball stadium not much farther in the same direction.

The pavilion we've entered is empty at this hour, sterile and surprisingly clean, with all its neon winking over a mile of vacant floor tile. We get coffee to go at Johnny Rockets, a faux-fifties diner with all its Pullman car decor stripped bare before this huge echoing space, like a Hollywood soundstage—and we take a long step back when the guy ahead of us drops his Big Gulp with a stupendous splash. This hypermodern setting could not be more alien to Benjamin Henry Latrobe, the architect who designed many Revolution-era structures in Baltimore and the region, and whose grandson, Ferdinand Claiborne Latrobe, was seven times mayor of Baltimore and Jack Heyrman's great-grandfather. Jack is telling me this because I asked, and as we leave the pavilion, blinking at the sudden brilliance of the sunlight reflected from the sequins of passing gangs of cheerleaders, he explains that the Latrobe lineage doesn't make much material difference in his life, since for one thing he doesn't have the name, and for another he doesn't think most people in Baltimore would recognize it nowadays. Cleveland Amory once said that Baltimore pays more honor to its fine old families than any American city, but you couldn't prove that by Jack, though he does find the Latrobe legends interesting, as do I.

Jack grew up in Baltimore, and spent most of the Vietnam years in Canada—though not, as it happens, to avoid the draft, for he already had conscientious objector status when he made the move. "I was tired of being an antiwar activist," he recalls. "Tired of the harassment, phone tapping, spying, et cetera, and to me, the alternative culture didn't look like much of a culture at all. So I had a chance to attend the University of New Brunswick in Canada, and I took it." A musician and music fan from early days, he returned to Baltimore in 1973, where he founded the Clean Cuts Music and Sound Design studio, which now has one busy operation in Baltimore's Hampden neighborhood, and two others still more bustling in the Washington, D.C., area. Clean Cuts isn't really a record company or label as such; its bread and butter is original scoring for TV and radio show and ads (plus similar sound tailoring for theaters and the Internet), but Jack has managed to release a few small jewels over the years, like a pair of solo piano records by his old friend Mac Rebennack, a.k.a. Dr. John.

Jack is at once an amiable guy and the angriest man I know. The stupidity, brutality, and wanton self-destructiveness of humankind upset him more than they do most people—therefore, it is safer not to get him started on the politics of our own time, but he can present the antics of Baltimore under the rule of Ferdinand Claiborne Latrobe as more amusing than horrifying.

Carefully, we cross Pratt Street again, plus a few lanes of Calvert Street that converge with it here; it is a distinctly pedestrian-unfriendly traverse, though there's not much traffic early on a Sunday morning. Halfway across, there is an oasis: an apron of brick named McKeldin

Square, in honor of Mayor Theodore McKeldin, who committed himself to revitalizing the Inner Harbor in 1963. Today, the area has a display of vaguely representational, brightly painted steel sculptures by Setsuko Ono, one of the few fine artists who is also a retiree from the World Bank. Among the sculptures are drifting more packs of muscular pint-sized young women in their warm-up jackets—one pair in glittery face-paint and cotton-candy-colored beehive hairdos that must be a homage to John Waters's inimitable Divine . . . though these two girls' insignia say they're from Maine. They're all attending a giant cheerleaders' competition down the block as it turns out, an event entitled, somewhat ominously, Final Destination.

We walk a block or so up Light Street, passing Burke's, whose atrocious mock-Tudor front belies (or perhaps correctly expresses) the classic Baltimore restaurant that lies within. Burke's has stood on the spot since 1934, and does a land-office business in burgers and basic seafood and fishbowls of beer. I sometimes get lunch at Burke's when I'm downtown, and I have the impression that most of the other people who eat there were born here. There's been a Comedy Factory upstairs for fifteen years or so, but this I have not had a good opportunity to sample.

Jack and I sit down on a bus-stop bench to finish our coffee. A bus pulls up and opens its doors, and once it's clear we're not getting on, the door hisses shut and the bus lumbers away up the hill. Never take a Number 3 bus uptown, Jack says automatically, because it turns east on Thirty-third Street and doesn't stop till it gets to Memorial Stadium (or where it used to be). He learned his way around Baltimore by bus, or on foot, because his mother didn't drive. In the mid-sixties, when he was in his teens, he and his friends used to catch the bus downtown to the Block (a string of show bars, once the venue for Blaze Starr, a little way east on Baltimore Street from where we're sitting now), attracted less by the strippers, he claims, than by the salient fact that Block bartenders seldom bothered to proof anybody. But for Jack, the real attraction of the Block was its pawnshops, which he could ransack for bargain guitars, and with that in mind we spend the next few minutes commiserating about how eBay has put so many pawn-shops out of business, especially the nice one on Red-wood Street, a little ways northwest of our bench, where you used to find brand-new Paul Reed Smith guitars for half price. Jack is appalled to learn (from me, since I recently tried to go there to replace a microphone in a hurry for a rehearsal at Gardel's) that Livingston's, the last of the Block pawnshops, has rolled down its gates for the last time.

Then we get up and toss our cups and walk a block east to Charles Street, the north-south artery that today runs from the Inner Harbor water line to the northern-most curve of the Baltimore Beltway. Charles, along with

Pratt Street, was originally named in honor of Charles Pratt, Earl of Camden, an Englishman who vigorously took the part of the American colonists as trouble with Britain brewed to a boil in the 1760s and 1770s. In the eighteenth century, Charles Street, with a different appearance than now, to be sure, ran up the west side of old Baltimore Town. No vestige of those old days remains on these lower blocks of the street today—the whole area was razed to the ground by the 1904 fire, and now is heavy on late-twentieth-century concrete pillboxes. South of the Lombard Street corner where we stand, Charles Street is flanked by a humongous Bank of America to the east, and to the west a towering skyscraper for the Legg Mason brokerage firm.

Jack and I bypass these financial fortresses, continuing north. Westward along Lombard Street, the Bromo-Seltzer clock tower rises, an Italianate campanile anomalous in this high-modern cityscape. Captain Isaac Emerson, the chemist who patented this medicine, decided to ornament his factory with a tower based on the one at Florence's Palazzo Vecchio. The enormous clock, once the largest in the world, still keeps time, and until 1936 a fifty-one-foot effigy of the Bromo-Seltzer bottle whirled on a pin above it. The grotesque incongruity of this combination would have been equally pleasing to John Waters or Edgar Allan Poe, but the late-twentieth-century clamor for the Blue Bottle's return has not so far been heeded.

For a moment, we pause in front of One Charles Center, a glass-walled high-rise designed by Mies van der Rohe, where Jack's father had an office during most of the time he worked for the Pinkerton detective service from 1959 to 1970. John Henry Heyrman hailed from Wisconsin. He served in the Army during the Depression, mustered out with the rank of sergeant, and turned himself into a private detective. When World War II started, he returned to military and served in the OSS under Wild Bill Donovan—he was one of two men in charge of counterinsurgency in areas the Allied invasion reclaimed as it swept across Europe. Discharged again at the end of the war, he started a detective agency in Chicago, working with one of the first fledgling credit card companies to trace defaulters and collect their debts. But he was still in the reserves, and in 1946 he was recalled to active duty. Passing through Baltimore on his way to rejoin the Army, he met Ann Aileen "Kitty" Latrobe, the eldest daughter of Ferdinand Claiborne Latrobe II.

The couple married on the island of Guam. Their eldest son, Jack, was born in Hokkaido, Japan. For the next several years, Jack and his mother followed his father from one military post to another, with occasional brief retreats to Baltimore, where Ann, Jack, and his younger brother, Peter (born in 1953), lived in one or another short-term rental around the north side of town. When John Henry Heyrman finally left the military and signed

on with the Pinkertons, he was able to live, at least theo-
retically, in Baltimore, though he traveled a lot for the
company—the main Pinkerton hub was in New York
City at that time. The Heyrman family settled permanently on Cloverhill Road, about five miles north of
where we're standing this morning, off Thirty-ninth
Street west of Charles.

From the corner of Redwood and Charles, we can
glimpse a section of the greened copper roof of the Lord
Baltimore Hotel and All-Caps Historic Landmark, built
in 1928, now operated by the Radisson hotel group.
Between us and the hotel is the former headquarters of
the B&O Railroad—critical in the days of Columbus
O'Donnell for distributing Canton's products and imports
overland into the Ohio Valley. The facade seems meant to
recall a Renaissance Florentine palazzo, and above the
keystone of the archway, Mercury and another curly
headed Roman god I am not personally acquainted with
cradle the globe between them—the North American
continent turned uppermost. The building was first
opened in 1906, just two years after Baltimore's great fire
destroyed the area where it stands, at midnight on September 12, with the simultaneous illumination of over
five thousand electric bulbs, and became an icon of Baltimore's determination to rebuild itself after the fire. But
over the next several decades, the B&O definitively lost
its battle with the Pennsylvania Railroad for dominance
of traffic along the east coast routes.

Debilitated by mergers since the 1960s, the B&O Railroad ceased to exist even in name in 1986. As the twentieth century neared its close, Maryland historian Frank R. Shivers Jr. described the building as "a giant tombstone of Baltimore's greatest business creation." Today, it's mostly occupied by law firms, with a BB&T bank on the ground floor. The vast lobby, two stories high and ornamented with marble staircases, stained-glass ceilings, and an enormous glittering chandelier, still conveys the overpowering opulence the original owners must have had in mind. A few months after Jack and I pass by, a one hundredth anniversary celebration of this monumental structure will be somewhat dampened by an imminent plan to raze and replace it with a prayer garden sponsored by the Catholic Archdiocese of Baltimore.

On the south side of Baltimore Street from the B&O mausoleum, the Morris A. Mechanic Theater occupies the site where the *Baltimore Sun* once had its press and its offices, in the days when H. L. Mencken and James M. Cain both worked there. The theater was designed by architect John M. Johansen according to what he called "functional expressionism," but was soon dubbed "Fort Mechanic" by unimpressed Baltimoreans. Johansen suggested that the outside of the building expressed the activities inside, which seems unjust, since the Mechanic is reputed to be one of the best theaters in the region.

Four blocks west, in Westminster Burying Ground, is the grave of Edgar Allan Poe, who died in Baltimore in

1849, after collapsing in the neighborhood of Ryan's Fourth Ward Polls, a voting station which also conveniently happened to be a tavern. Poe spent a long season in Baltimore with his first wife, Virginia Clemm, and her mother, who also happened to be his aunt—the three of them shared a tiny brick house on Amity Street in West Baltimore, now operated as a museum by the city of Baltimore, and surrounded by suitably melancholy urban slums that have since grown up around it.

After Virginia's death from tuberculosis, Poe returned to Richmond, where he had spent most of his orphaned childhood. He was engaged to be married again to a friend of his youth, the recently widowed Sarah Shelton, when he sailed out of Richmond with the somewhat unusual object of fetching his first wife's mother from her home in the Bronx to attend his wedding to the second bride. The ship out of Richmond made port in Baltimore, and Poe went missing for several days; certainly he never appeared in New York, though he may have got as far as Philadelphia. In the midst of elections on October 3, someone recognized him in the Fourth Ward Polls (a.k.a. Cooth & Sergeant's Tavern), where he had collapsed in a state of delirium or drunkenness, and appeared to be wearing someone else's clothes. He was duly taken to a hospital, but died in a few days' time without ever recovering his clarity of mind or explaining what had happened to him. The most usual explanation is that Poe (most unpredictably, given the happy turn his personal life was taking) had simply gone on a suicidal bender. A variation suggests that he was plied with drink by electioneers and dragged from one polling place to another for multiple voting purposes (which might explain the change of clothes). But since Poe's death has never been fully explained, it still attracts exotic theories: He might have slipped into a diabetic coma, for example, or suddenly come down with acute disseminated encephalomyelitis.

In fact, Poe has two graves in Westminster Burying Ground, since his remains were moved from a plot at the rear of the small graveyard to a place of greater honor near the front gate, at the corner of Fayette and Greene Streets. The monument there, funded by a long slow dribble of contributions from Baltimore schoolchildren, was described by the ever-charitable H. L. Mencken as "cheap and hideous." Poe himself was "a genius," Mencken somewhat grudgingly acknowledged, while in the same breath calling him "a foolish, disingenuous, and often somewhat trashy man." Presiding over the unveiling of the monument in 1875, John H. B. Latrobe (who had met Poe briefly some forty years before, when serving on a committee that awarded Poe his first literary prize: $50 for "MS. Found in a Bottle") took a more respectful view: "Gentleman was written all over him. His manner was easy and quiet. . . . " Whatever its aesthetic qualities, Poe's monument still occasionally sprouts flowers and other offerings from mysteriously haunted donors; the Edgar Allan Poe Society officially lays a

wreath there on the first Sunday in October, the approx-
imate anniversary of Poe's death.

Jack and I keep on walking, rather sharply uphill—
the statue atop the Washington Monument, some distance ahead, appears between the tall buildings lining
Charles Street like a bead centered in the notch of a
gunsight. Here at the corner of Lexington, Charles Street
narrows drastically. We turn back and look over the mul-
tilane roadway that spills back down the harbor's edge.
The 1904 fire stopped more or less where we're standing,
leaving acres of scorched earth available for new construction. The high-rises that sprouted out of those ashes
eventually closed off the views of the harbor that the
older building on the low hills farther north along
Charles Street had formerly enjoyed.

Here, too, on the west side of the street, O'Neill's
Department Store once flourished, an emporium that
employed Ann Aileen Latrobe and most of her friends
when they were in their teens. Though less august than
some other downtown department stores of its day,
O'Neill's benefited from its spot at the end of the Number 4 and 14 streetcar lines, and both its customers and
salespeople were loyal for the long haul. Built in 1882, the
store folded in 1955, and the building was torn down to
make way for new construction.

On the northwest corner of Lexington there is a
truly heavyweight stone building, towering many stories
into the shrinking downtown sky, whose masonry

reminds me at first glance of the Flatiron Building in New York. Built to house the Fidelity and Deposit insurance company in 1893, it's commonly known as the Fidelity Building, and was one of the few buildings in the area to survive the Great Fire of 1904 (which stopped just short of it). This building housed the Abell Company, parent to the *Baltimore Sun* until 1986 when the Sun papers were sold to the Times-Mirror newspaper consortium. For some years thereafter, the Fidelity Building continued to shelter the Abell Foundation, which has a $150 million endowment to do imaginative good works among the city's too numerous poor. Now quartered a couple of blocks east on Howard Street, the Abell Foundation supports programs in health, education, employment, conservation, and the environment, to name only a few of the pies into which it has inserted a beneficent finger.

It sort of hurts my neck to crane back to peer at the top of the Fidelity Building. I roll my head and we keep climbing, to a little summit where Cathedral Street runs diagonally into Charles from the northwest. There we pause in the shade of the triple arched portico of Old Saint Paul's basilica, the first bastion of the Anglican Episcopal church in Baltimore, though not the first building to house it. Four churches have stood on this site since 1739, and the ground was allotted to Saint Paul's Parish in the first survey of Baltimore Town in 1730.

Baltimore and the state of Maryland were founded, by the Calvert family of England, on principles of religious tolerance somewhat unusual for the time, inspired by considerable experience of religious intolerance. George Calvert was secretary to Sir Robert Cecil, himself a close councillor of King James I of England (and VI of Scotland). Calvert became a favorite of King James, but in 1625 he disclosed that he was in fact a Catholic and accordingly resigned his post. King James (who himself had renounced Catholicism for Anglicanism so as to gain the English throne) compensated George Calvert with a fief that included the town of Baltimore in Ireland; Calvert thus became the first Lord Baltimore. Turning his eye on the New World, he picked a tract of land north of the colony of Virginia by circling it on the map, but died, in 1632, before King James could grant him a charter for it.

His son, Cecil Calvert, the second Lord Baltimore, received Maryland's first charter and organized the first expedition of colonists in 1633 under the leadership of his brother Leonard. Cecil Calvert had it in mind (as his father also may have done) to create a haven for Catholics in the New World, but he needed to make these arrangements discreetly. The "Instructions to the Colonists" that Cecil composed became the basis of Maryland's first laws, and the document included this prescription: "be very careful to preserve unity and peace amongst the passengers . . . and that they suffer no scandall nor offence to be given to any of the Protestants . . . all Acts of Romane Catholique Religion to be done as privately as may be, and that they instruct all Romane Catholiques to be silent upon all occasions concerning matters of Religion." The majority of the first colonists were Anglicans, but the leaders were Catholic, and Cecil took precautions that the colony should not fracture over religious dissent. England itself came very close to doing so during the Catholic-Protestant civil war that went on from 1642 to 1649.

Some of that sectarian strife did reach Maryland, but Cecil's foresight paid off and he was able to retain control of the colony by appointing a Protestant governor. In 1649, he proposed an Act Concerning Religion, more commonly known as the Act of Toleration, which allowed the practice of any Christian faith, so long as citizens were loyal to the civil government—an important forerunner of the U.S. constitutional guarantee of religious freedom. The Maryland Assembly voted this act into law, and Cecil Calvert's son Charles, who came to govern Maryland in 1661, maintained the principle until the 1680s, when the new Protestant rulers of England, William and Mary, stripped him of the colony . . . because he was a Catholic.

In the midst of this snakes-and-ladders game of religious ascendancy, Saint Paul's was first chartered by the Church of England in 1692, and originally occupied a log cabin where the Dundalk neighborhood is today. Soon after Baltimore Town was chartered, the church moved to where it is now. After the third church on this site burned down in 1854, architect Richard Upjohn designed the present structure—a mostly brick structure, with imposing marble columns lining the front portico. Upjohn's original plan included a nine-story campanile; if it had ever been built, one could from its height still capture a clear view of the harbor. The place we're standing is the highest point inside the original limits of eighteenth-century Baltimore Town. Jack points at the 1st Mariner Bank building, dovetailed into the triangular plot on the northwest corner of Cathedral and Charles, and lets me know that back in the day few buildings were taller than its five stories; today, in 2006, the harbor view from this hilltop is mostly obstructed by the high-rises along lower Charles.

A couple of blocks farther north, we happen upon Clayton & Co.—"Coffee and Tea, Fine Books" emblazoned on a new black and gold sign, below the emblems of the former tenant, whose shingle has been painted over in the strikingly dark maroon of the whole facade: "Lycett Stationers, Importers, Engravers." I have been meaning to visit Clayton's for a long time, since I have known the owner off and on for many years: Cameron Northouse, before he started his present enterprise, ran a distinguished small publishing house under his family name. For most of the twenty-plus years I have lived here, Baltimore has been somewhat underserved by bookstores. In the mid-eighties, the best choice in town was Louie's Bookstore Café in the dip just south of the

Washington Monument. A favorite watering hole for all the local literati, it was mostly a restaurant and had little shelf space, though it made the most of what it did have. A few years later, local entrepreneurs founded an independent superstore, Bibelot, on an acre-wide floor plan in Timonium, a township on York Road just north of the Baltimore Beltway. The reception was so enthusiastic at first that Bibelot quickly added several more warehouse stores at strategic points all over town, vacuuming up practically all of Baltimore's bookselling talent and, incidentally, putting a number of smaller independent operations out of business. Ever more dangerously overextended, Bibelot collapsed under its own weight in 2001, and in a noir twist somewhat unusual for the book business, the owners did their best to move their assets out of the country, transferring some $20 million to an offshore trust perkily christened "Book Worm Too."

Since then, the chain superstores have moved into the vacuum, and Barnes & Noble has survived the best in this latest round of literary Darwinism, with a megastore in the Power Plant complex on the Inner Harbor, another on a hilltop in Towson (a township tucked just south of the beltway on York Road), and a third under construction in Charles Village, a few miles north of where we are now. So there are a lot more books for sale in Baltimore than there used to be, but still, a new independent store is a beautiful sight to behold, and Claytons & Co. is exquisite in every detail. Full of books that excite the most powerful covetousness (collectible first editions for the most part), it is also beautifully laid out and decorated, even down to the restroom, where memorabilia hung on the rich red walls includes three matchbox-sized purses that the belles of another era must have carried to their balls, and a small portrait of Jane Morris, muse to the Pre-Raphaelite painters—Dante Gabriel Rossetti in particular, who painted this image as a sketch for La Donna della Finestra—centered between two other beauties of her time.

Northouse and his wife, Donna, are manning a nice-looking café counter, with an array of coffee concoctions to put Starbucks to shame, and a nice selection of fresh pastries to tempt the passerby. I wish I had got my coffee here, instead of Harborplace—it surely would have been much better coffee. But we plan to be on the street for a good many more miles and several more hours, which means that fluid intake must be monitored with an eye to its eventual consequences. Cameron and I do a little scheming about events the store might host for Goucher creative writing students in the fall. After that, Jack and I go on our way.

As we hit the street, Jack observes that nice as the store is, the problem it faces is . . . there aren't any passersby to speak of. Indeed, we have met practically no one during our walk so far. Of course, it is early on Sunday morning, in an era when the churches don't draw like they used to, but Jack says that even during the week, foot traffic in the area has become very thin—a dearth of up-and-running office buildings in the area has starved out most of the retail.

It wasn't like that when Jack was a kid. The parallel stretch of Howard Street a couple of blocks west was lined with Baltimore's finest department stores: Stewart's, Hochschild Kohn's, Hutzler's, and Hecht's (all of them dead as the dinosaurs now so far as Howard Street is concerned, though Hecht's still has a store in the Towson mall) and if you showed grace under the pressure of clothes shopping, if you behaved like a good boy, why, then you might be brought over to Charles Street afterward, to have lunch at the Women's Industrial Exchange, founded in the nineteenth century as a place where gentlewomen in straitened circumstances might discreetly sell needlework and comestibles. The place kept going as a shop and restaurant long after the notion of proper women engaging in commerce had ceased to be problematic, and closed its doors, to the regret of its many breakfast and lunch consumers, just a few years ago.

A block or so up from Clayton & Co., we stop in front of the narrow archway of Brown's Arcade—Baltimore's first indoor shopping mall, created in 1910 by Governor Frank Brown, out of four early nineteenth-century row houses. Jack used to play Rotisserie baseball here, in what was probably the first such fantasy league in Baltimore. Founded by a part-time bartender at Pacifica

Restaurant in the arcade, Stan "the fan" Charles (who to this day posts Baltimore sports stories on the World Wide Web) brought wine merchant Mitch Pressman, filmmaker Brian Keller, and philosopher Steve Vicchio, among many others, into one of the more strikingly inclusive Rotisserie leagues in the city. Today, Brown's Arcade is indicated both by a sign in the pediment above the door and by tile work on the floor between the entry columns. There's one florist operating inside the short corridor, and upstairs if you so desire you may check out Rock to the Rescue Bail Bonds, but the other couple of arcade storefronts are empty till you get to the back. Here a greenhouse roof covers what must once have been a queer little open courtyard, where the backs of four small houses met to surround an irregular space of cobbles. It's a restful place, and there are benches here, and one of the crookedly joined facades promotes an Irish pub called Tir Nan Og, only you have to go around outside the arcade to get into it, for Tir Nan Og today is the snug of a larger operation, Mick O'Shea's.

Low hills go rippling north from the harbor, and by walking up a constantly gentle grade we have gradually acquired a little altitude, without really noticing it. Now we descend a little dip to Pleasant Street, and then we are mounting the southside of a steeper rise, which, according to Jack, few people call Cathedral Hill anymore. In the days when more people traveled by shank's mare, this approach via Charles Street was also called

Cardiac Hill, thanks to its near-vertical pitch. At the top, on the northwest corner of Mulberry Street, the Basilica of the National Shrine of the Assumption of the Blessed Virgin Mary is covered in scaffolding, in the course of a major renovation, which will among other things let new light into the interior by repairing the skylights that circle the dome; these have been covered over for decades, Jack tells me, most likely because they leaked. Dark as a tomb for a very long time, the basilica is due for a burst of great illumination.

America's French allies camped on this hill in 1781—Generals Washington and Rochambeau strategized here, on the eve of the Battle of Yorktown. Some twenty years later (with Catholicism again permitted in Maryland, thanks to the Revolution), Benjamin Henry Latrobe was appointed architect for construction of the cathedral. His cross-shaped plan was ambitious for the time and place, calling for a sixty-five-foot-high barrel vault, and a double dome at the crossing. Today, his great-great-great-grandson reminds me that, throughout the nineteenth century, this hilltop, too, had a clear view down to the harbor. Seen from shipboard in those days, the cathedral was thought by some to resemble the hilltop mosques of the East, and its dome was the principal Baltimore landmark for sailors coming into the port.

Fanny Trollope, a visitor to Baltimore in the 1830s, was much taken with the beauty of the cathedral and the impression made by its dome from a distance. The mother of the novelist Anthony Trollope had entered the United States by way of New Orleans, then spent a couple of years in Cincinnati (which she felt had been all too rapidly converted from a "bear-brake" into a "prosperous city"). Baltimore gave her a first glimpse, in the New World, of the sort of European civilization for which she pined: "Baltimore is, I think, one of the handsomest cities to approach in the Union. The noble column erected to the memory of Washington, and the Catholic cathedral, with its beautiful dome, being built on a commanding eminence, are seen at a great distance. As you draw nearer, many other domes and towers become visible, and as you enter Baltimore-street, you feel that you are arrived in a handsome and populous city."

The basilica fronts on Cathedral Street, which explains how Cathedral Street got its name, facing the almost equally stately Enoch Pratt Free Library there. We are passing the back of it now, and the cardinal's residence in the rear, with its stately facade facing Charles Street. This house, completed in 1829, provides all the prelates who occupy it with a covered and private passage to the rear of the cathedral. It's a striking structure, flanked by two wings, and with its alternation pattern of blue-gray and off-white stone somewhat recalling the palette of Wedgwood china. Today, the residence faces Sotta Sopra across Charles Street, which offers high-end Italian cuisine in a gorgeously opulent setting, whose details include bigger-than-life murals on the mirrors depicting

2-D diners enjoying much the same menu as you are. Next door is An die Musik, an esoteric record store that moved downtown from Towson years ago, and which has a small performance space for sophisticated chamber acts that pass through town.

And now we go down the north side of Cathedral Hill. In that next trough, on the northwest corner of Franklin Street, is the white domed cube of Baltimore's first Unitarian church, completed by the French architect Maximilien Godefroy in 1818, at a moment when Unitarianism was gaining ground across the eastern seaboard. Two prominent members of the church were philanthropists George Peabody and Enoch Pratt, who founded the Free Library a block east. Jared Sparks, the first pastor of the Franklin Street church, served later on as chaplain of Congress and president of Harvard University. The terra-cotta Angel of Truth sculpted by Antonio Capellano when the church was built stands out sharply in a reddish-brown clay nimbus in the central pediment above the doors, while below a black on white sign affixed to the black iron railing reads, "Against stupidity, the gods themselves struggle in vain." Acoustics under the dome were so terrible, Jack tells me as we go past, that finally the Unitarians had to install a dropped ceiling to make the sermons intelligible.

I shoot a quick look to the east on Franklin Street, toward Teo Pepe's, long reputed to be Baltimore's most expensive restaurant, and certainly one of its best. As we pass the corner, I do a double take when I glance to my right and see letters on a plate-glass window that seem to read, "ERASURE OF THE TEXT BOOKSTORE"—which seems very postmodern for Baltimore. But on second glance, I realize that the first *R* in "ERASURE" has slipped in through some fissure in my brain, and Jack, peering more closely through our reflections on the glass, makes out the ghost of a stenciled *P* and *L*. The sign should thus read "PLEASURE OF THE TEXT BOOKSTORE" . . . but the store itself does seem to have been erased, and the room behind the glass is empty.

Another glance to the right reveals a couple of small brick Federal-style houses surviving at the corner of Hamilton and North Lovegrove Streets, their spotless marble steps framed by iron railings and gleaming in the morning sun. These simple buildings go back to the 1830s, when they stood on the fringe of the swank Mount Vernon neighborhood. As we climb toward the Washington Monument, we pass a building faced with much more elaborate ironwork—porch and the narrow balcony above faced in elaborate vine-leaf filigree, the sight of which recalls to Jack that most of the ironwork in New Orleans' French quarter was originally manufactured here in Baltimore.

We've sailed over another ripple of earth and are going down past the storefront where Louie's has lately been replaced by **X** (so designated, its signs proclaim it to be a jazz and blues club; its menu offers semi-French cuisine), into another dip at Centre Street and the southern foot of Washington Place. On our right hand is the Buttery restaurant, just recently boarded up. "Used to be a good place to go get poisoned," Jack snarls briefly, as we pause on the corner. Me, I never got around to trying it, and now it's too late. Straight ahead and above us, an equestrian bronze of Lafayette seems to leading a charge downhill from the next height, where Washington, clad in Roman toga and laurel wreath, stands atop a towering pillar inspired (it is said) by the Column of Trajan in Rome. If we had the energy, we could go in the door at the base of the column and climb 228 steps to rejoice in a truly panoramic view. We don't.

West along Centre Street is the Walters Art Museum, originally based on the donations of William Thompson Walters and his son Henry, fanatical art collectors who sat out the Civil War in Paris, acquiring French paintings of such importance as to make the Walters collection competitive with major museums all over the world. But the founders did not limit themselves to French classic painting; they also collected Asian art, armor, Fabergé eggs, medieval Italian religious painting, Louis XIV furniture, and various other objets d'art, for a total of roughly twenty-five thousand, many of them displayed in a new wing to the museum at the corner of Centre and Cathedral Street. The original building, a nineteenth-century mansion fronting on Charles Street to the left of where we're standing now, was left to the city along with the collection by Henry Walters when he died. The Asian component of the Walters collection (some of it, at least) is to be found in Hackerman House, an 1850s mansion a short way to the north. West of Hackerman House, at 5 Mount Vernon Place, is the Walters family home—no slouch of a mansion in its own right, though it is outdone in extravagance by the tremendous brownstone built by Mary Frick Garrett Jacobs next door.

The park surrounding the Washington Monument is laid out in the symmetrical form of a Greek cross draped over the point of the hill. Two blocks' worth of green space extends north-south along Charles Street (here called Washington Avenue) and east-west along the much shorter Monument Street (here called Mount Vernon Place). The land once belonged to John Eager Howard's Belvedere estate; his great grandfather, George Eager, bought the tract from Lord Baltimore in 1688. Howard was a Revolutionary comrade and friend of George Washington, and he donated the ground for the monument in 1809, after a deal for a downtown site was queered by householders' concern that the colossal column might topple and crush their dwellings. That might just as well happen here and now, but when construction on the monument began, there were no other buildings nearby.

Robert Mills designed both the monument itself and the Greek-cross pattern of Mount Vernon Square.

Credited with being the United States' first native architect, Mills learned much of his craft from assisting Thomas Jefferson in building projects at Monticello. He won the commission for the Baltimore monument in a design contest, and went on to erect the 555-foot-high railroad spike in Washington's honor on the Mall of the nation's capital. Between monuments, Mills also designed Waterloo Row, one of the first blocks of row houses flanking Mount Vernon Square on the far side of Saint Paul Street from the monument—a row demolished in the 1960s, and replaced with an apartment house.

It was Howard's heirs who gave additional land for the streets that radiate from the column, they who sagaciously laid out the first building lots along those promenades. Antebellum mansions began to mushroom alongside the four arms of the Greek-cross plan, and once the nation began to recover from the Civil War, a second wave of opulent building began. Mount Vernon, now populated by railroad barons and other commercial lords of the 1890s, became the nexus of Baltimore's Gilded Age. A tacit understanding that no structure should be higher than the monument was all that limited these two bursts of growth.

Some of the railroad barons, also sometimes called robber barons, were moved to appease their consciences with philanthropic acts. Along with the Walters Art Museum, the arts center founded by George Peabody in the 1850s has earned the southern area of Mount Vernon square the sobriquet "Culture Corner." Peabody was less an industrialist than a pure financier, who rose from an impoverished childhood in New England through twenty years in a Baltimore dry-goods operation to become so powerful a force in the City of London that he was able to bolster the failing credit of the Union during the Civil War. Peabody's gifts have been significant all over the country. In Baltimore, he was determined to erect his institution right on the edge of Washington Monument. The original Peabody Institute building went up on the southwest side of Mount Vernon Place in the 1860s; the adjacent library followed during the next decade. Today, the Peabody Conservatory remains one of the best music schools in the region. George Peabody sent an architect from England (where he himself would finish his days), and the original buildings, designed by Edmund Lind in Renaissance Revival style, are part of Baltimore's architectural pride. Mr. Peabody himself, firmly cast in bronze, is relaxing (though weightily) in an armchair in the eastern arm of the Mount Vernon cross, just in front of the glorious building he paid for.

Jack and I are still taking a breather at the foot of Washington Place, beneath General Lafayette's bronze advance, gazing at a lovely little bronze nymphette who poses on top a stippled hemisphere that looks rather like a sea urchin, in the center of a fountain encircled by stone stairs that swirl up toward the base of Washington's column. The grassy promenades around the monument, now open to the public 24-7, were not always so: in the Roaring Nineties, they were locked up in iron fencing, except for special occasions when Mayor Ferdinand Latrobe would open the gates and let in throngs of excited children.

Today, Jack Heyrman is telling me that John Quincy Adams once referred to Baltimore as "the Monumental City." Since the Washington Monument had not yet been built, he wasn't talking about that; but Baltimore, which in Jack's view already suffered from a sense of being second rate as compared with Washington, New York, and Boston, was inspired by Adams's casual remark to raise more monuments—and lots of them, too. The cross arms of Mount Vernon Square are festooned with them like ornaments on a Christmas tree, including but not limited to statues of Supreme Court chief justice Roger Brook Taney, Severn Teakle Wallis (the lawyer famous for resisting the Know-Nothing party in the 1850s), and, charging up Charles Street from the north end of Washington Place, the equestrian John Eager Howard himself, in a martial pose commemorating his performance at the Battle of Cowpens, where he is said to have captured seven British swords.

Rested now, Jack and I resume the climb, passing the naiad poised on her urchin and circling the cobblestones fanning out from the base of the column in a counterclockwise direction. On the corner posts of the stone barrier to our right are two small bronzes representing classical warriors, wreathed in laurel but not much more, embracing wild beasts and their weapons, and somewhat ominously labeled "FORCE" and "ORDER." In the two o'clock position, on the northeast corner of Washington and Mount Vernon Place, once stood an 1829 mansion belonging to John Eager Howard's son Charles. There Francis Scott Key, whose daughter was married to Charles Howard, died in 1843. The 1829 house gave way in 1872 to the Mount Vernon Place United Methodist Church, constructed of a curious greenish stone in a Victorian Gothic style, with delicate spires reminiscent of a Disneyland castle.

On the next block, we pause and gaze across the greensward at the old Stafford Hotel—a swank address, when it opened in the 1890s, for honeymooners and for some Baltimoreans who spent the coldest winter months there, in retreat from drafty shingled houses in north-side neighborhoods like Roland Park. F. Scott Fitzgerald (named for his far distant ancestor, the anthem-writing Francis Scott Key) was also a regular at the Stafford during its prime. Later in the twentieth century, the hotel went into decline, and in 1970 was converted into subsidized housing for the elderly. Though the building is now (again) a prime piece of real estate, Jack figures it is doomed for the otherwise logical development into luxury condos . . . because it has no parking. Signs in the window today suggest that it provides housing to area students, from the Peabody Conservatory or from Johns

Hopkins University and the Maryland Institute, to the north and northwest.

Conceived and executed as the city's most desirable neighborhood (Jérôme Bonaparte had a house here, as well as the Howards and the Walters and the Carrolls and so many other Baltimore gentry), Mount Vernon began to slip slightly down-market, at least in certain blocks, as early as the 1890s, when the first grand mansions (which required many servants, not to say slaves, to operate and maintain) began to be converted into boardinghouses serving a more transient population. In Baltimore's checkerboard scheme of small and contiguous "good" and "bad" neighborhoods, a small area like Mount Vernon can be quickly eroded. If there wasn't so much stuff in the way, Jack and I could look a mere three blocks northeast and read the banner recently hung high above the hum of the Jones Falls Expressway on the outer walls of the old penitentiary, now Central Booking, in square black letters on a maroon background:

PUT DOWN THE GUN
OR PICK A ROOM

It's not exactly poetry, but it is a clear statement, and in its own terse way it represents, one might say, the nadir of the boardinghouse lifestyle.

But Mount Vernon has come back from its mild episode of urban blight. A gay community, attracted by the period architecture and by the cultural institutions that never stopped functioning, has played a part in stabilizing the neighborhood and making it safe. Once again, this neighborhood has become a highly desirable (and quite expensive) place to live. Since the day of its completion, the Washington Monument has been a rallying point in times of public crisis and of public celebration. Today, the tall column serves as a maypole for events like the Baltimore Book Festival, which has filled Mount Vernon Square with books and bibliophiles every fall for the last decade. We are here just a little too late to catch the May Flower Mart, which covers all these promenades with bloom, and which Jack remembers as the main Mount Vernon event of his childhood. He thought of it then as the last gasp of the Old South (Baltimore being as much a southern town as anything else), because of the women he used to see wearing fancy hats and long dresses as they browsed the flowers. "If you saw something like that now," he says, "you'd think they were shooting a movie."

We keep moving, leaving the top arm of the grassy Greek cross, glancing west along Madison Street (no relation) toward the brownstone Gothic sandcastle spire of the First and Franklin Street Presbyterian Church. Its congregation first gathered in a log meetinghouse in 1761; the present and very handsome edifice was designed by the architect N. G. Starkweather and completed in 1875.

There's a pocket of ethnic restaurants on the blocks going down the north slope from Monument Hill: sushi, Vietnamese, and, down a set of iron-railed steps, the Akbar Indian restaurant, which puts on a fantabulous lunch buffet (and charges practically nothing for it). The blue and white Greek restaurant, Never on Sunday, is closed, of course, because it's Sunday. Though I've never eaten there, to me it's sort of a landmark (well, it's been there as long as I've been in Baltimore), but to Jack it's nowhere near so venerable. In hippie times, he lets me know, the place was popular as the Earl of Sandwich sandwich shop. To our left is Helmand, the Afghan restaurant, which by virtue of its excellent food, agreeable atmosphere, and reasonable prices had built a loyal following, in the eighties and nineties, among Baltimoreans who in those days knew zip about Afghanistan beyond perhaps some cloudy conception of gaunt, heroic mujahideen fighting off the Soviets, maybe sorta like American revolutionaries fighting off the redcoats, but after September 11 the local conception of mujahideen suddenly and drastically changed and the owners and operators of Helmand had to do some fast, urgent explanation of the point that *they* in fact had no interest or sympathy in the Taliban or terrorism and indeed had a record of opposing both . . . all of which was perfectly true, to the point that Helmand's owner is the brother of Hamid Karzai, the post-invasion, post-Taliban, Afghan head of state.

Jack cocks his head at the building now, telling me that it is generally called Park Plaza for some reason, and that there used to be a club upstairs from the restaurant space where Emmylou Harris sometimes performed back when she was just a semipro folksinging long-haired girl on the club beat here and in D.C., before her first duets with Gram Parsons had set her on the road to country-music stardom. Read Street, which we are now approaching, was hippie central, according to Jack, back in whatever set of years gets lumped under the label "the sixties," with the usual beads and bangles and tie-dyes and black lights and posters and record stores and head shops and all, radiating across Read and up and down Charles, and the upper floors of the row houses we are passing now had morphed into hippie crash pads where a good number of Jack's friends lived then.

The Latrobe building on the northeast corner of Read is not the same mansion at 906 North Charles Street where Ferdinand Claiborne Latrobe lived during most of his long reign as mayor—though it does occupy the same spot, just across Read Street from another fine house (901 North Charles Street) where the mayor's mother, Charlotte Virginia Claiborne Latrobe, then resided. Charlotte Virginia Claiborne descended from a William Claiborne, who purchased and settled Kent Island in the late 1620s—later on, however, his possession came into conflict with the Calvert's land grant, and the Calverts did their best to have him hanged as a pirate.

William Claiborne finally abandoned Maryland for Virginia, and his descendants migrated to Mississippi. Charlotte Virginia Claiborne was born and raised in Natchez, and met her husband, John Hazelhurst de Boneval Latrobe (son of the architect Benjamin), at the White Sulphur Springs resort in West Virginia. After their wedding, they returned to Baltimore on horseback, by a route which in those days passed through hostile Indian territory.

Like many Baltimoreans of her time, Charlotte Latrobe sympathized strongly with the Confederacy— her son Osmun Latrobe was a colonel in the Confederate army—but she was also strong enough for Southern hospitality to receive the Federal general B. F. "Beast" Butler as a house guest at the Latrobe's country estate outside Baltimore. On his departure, Butler offered her any favor he could render, and two years later she took him up on it, asking Butler to get a pair of boots to her son. "Beast" Butler's reply informed her that "it was the business of his army to kill all the Confederates they could, and her son among them, if possible"; he did, however, deliver the boots, and got a written receipt for them.

"A man of methodical habits," Ferdinand Latrobe (forever known for some reason as "General Latrobe") crossed Read Street every morning to have breakfast with his mother, and when she died in 1903, he continued to take the morning meal with his sister, who also lived at 901 North Charles Street. His breakfast accomplished, General Latrobe had only to trundle a couple of blocks north on Charles to the Maryland Club, to cluster with his cronies there. The bartender there was Latrobe's good friend, and though perhaps not an exact double for the mayor at close quarters, was of the same physical type, large and rotund, and wore the same handlebar mustache, so that on days when General Latrobe was fatigued by the demands of the public, he could lend the bartender his mayoral costume and send him to various large functions in his stead. So long as the bartender only waved and bowed and smiled and was careful not to say too much and careful not to stay too long, no one was ever the wiser.

In the days before mass media, Jack explains, and especially before television, this kind of public appearance (in authentic person or by stand-in proxy) was hugely important to maintaining the mayor's popularity and prestige, and this in an era when the mayor's office was far more powerful than that of the governor, since most of the population of Maryland was concentrated in Baltimore. For the same reason, General Latrobe would dress in his finest every Sunday and spend the day driving around Baltimore in a horse-drawn carriage, greeting the people he passed on the street. The object was not only to be seen but also to see—to see for oneself—and ever since then, Jack tells me, "it was considered important in my family to go up and down streets and know about stuff."

On the blocks between Latrobe House and the Maryland Club, we stop to look at two plain brick three-story Federal row houses. One houses the Brass Elephant on its ground floor—one of Baltimore's longest-lived fine restaurants, and even from across the street we can see that all its tables have already been laid with blindingly white starched linen. Next door, there's a more recent arrival, which looks, perhaps, a touch more casual: Mughal Garden Restaurant & Bar. The stories above the Brass Elephant are very plain, the windows completely unadorned excepting their white marble sills and lintels. The windows over the Mughal Garden are slightly more ornate, decorated with concrete scrolls on either side. In the days when Baltimore clippers ruled the world of trade, Jack tells me, houses in these blocks belonged to merchants and shipowners, and all of these houses had ironwork balconies where the merchants could display their exotic wares—back when all Baltimore was a sail-powered town. The nimble speed of the small light clippers was the despair of the British navy during the War of 1812, when the clippers could outmaneuver any British attempt at a blockade.

The Maryland Club still stands on the corner of Eager Street, a heavyweight, gloomy, gray stone edifice. We pass it by, nearing the center of John Eager Howard's grand estate. Here, when he married at the Revolution's victorious close, he built a mansion in the center of a property that was generally known as Howard's Belvedere.

Times have changed since those pastoral days. As it runs toward the eastern perimeter of Howard's old holding, Eager Street now passes along the north wall of the old penitentiary, today's Central Booking, and plunges into the scariest of the eastside slums.

John Eager Howard's wife, whom he courted by the proxy of the doctor treating him for his Revolutionary war wounds, was born and raised in Philadelphia. Née Peggy Chew, as Mrs. Howard she turned the Belvedere mansion Howard built for her into the principal hub around which Baltimore's high society revolved. When a north-moving construction boom advanced into what had been Howard's country estate, Howard's mansion went under the wave. The present Belvedere Hotel, built in 1903 on the corner of Charles and Chase Street, became the new high-society center, where mint juleps or pink ladies were far more likely to be imbibed than tea. Baltimore debutantes were launched from the Belvedere dance floor. At a party he gave here for his daughter Scotty, F. Scott Fitzgerald, somewhat the worse for drink that evening, unnerved a number of the girls by insisting on dancing with them.

When he was seventeen years old, Jack Heyrman picketed the Belvedere Hotel—that was in 1966, and he and his group were protesting the campaign of George P. Mahoney, a pavement contractor who was running for governor against Spiro Agnew, and specifically against the open-housing provisions of President Johnson's civil rights bill. Mahoney sent sound trucks all around Baltimore blasting his slogan: "Your Home Is Your Castle—Protect It!" The right to racial discrimination in real-estate sales was what Mahoney was out to defend—in an era when George Wallace could bring home 42.7 percent of the popular presidential vote in Maryland. At the end of the day, Mahoney lost to Agnew (formerly Anagnostopoulos), but not before inspiring his opponent to challenge Maryland voters to choose between "the courageous flame of righteousness and the evil of a fiery cross"— one of Agnew's first metaphorical extravagances to make it into the public record.

The picketers packed up their signs and left, and the Belvedere Hotel drifted into the doldrums; it no longer has its one-and-only-accept-no-substitutes significance in Baltimore social hierarchy. Emily Post, who rose to her social arbiter's throne from more modest beginnings in her father's house nearby on Chase Street, has long since yielded her scepter to the far less dogmatic, more ecumenical Miss Manners. As social structures begin to dissolve, the edifices that gave them a stage begin to lose some of their aura; still, the Belvedere Hotel remains an imposing building, dominating the city skyline from almost any approach—for many years it was the tallest building in Baltimore. In 1992, the Belvedere converted its last hotel rooms into condos, but the top-floor cocktail lounge is still open to the public, and so is the famous Owl Bar, right on the ground floor.

Invited to donate the Belvedere estate for a public park on the scale of Patterson or Druid Hill Park or Central Park in New York City, the heirs and assigns of John Eager Howard preferred to open it to residential development instead. And so the wave of Renaissance Revival building, among other elaborate architectural styles, rolled farther north up Charles Street and the surrounding blocks. Here lived the Baltimore aristocracy that built the B&O Railroad, and traveled on it, using the Mount Royal Station just a few blocks northeast, a long, handsome stone building with an elegant Italianate clock tower and sumptuous waiting rooms that set the standard for first-class voyaging. The Baltimore aristocracy founded northside neighborhoods like Roland Park as summer communities (at first), and in that same northern area they launched Baltimore's first private prep schools, like Calvert, Boys' Latin, and the Bryn Mawr School, the latter founded by the classical scholar Edith Hamilton and a few other like-minded people with the purpose of preparing girls—exclusively—to attend Bryn Mawr College in Pennsylvania, at a time when few other opportunities for higher education were open to women at all. For this community, the Jones Falls was their River Lethe; they crossed it to eternal rest in Greenmount Cemetery a few blocks east.

Betsy Patterson Bonaparte, who now reposes in that cemetery with most of the rest of her generation of Baltimore gentry, first retreated to a fine house a block west on Cathedral Street, following the collapse of her marriage to the emperor's younger brother, Jérôme. She was eighteen, and he only nineteen, when they met and married, and Napoléon Bonaparte, ruthless in love as he was in war, simply had the marriage annulled. In the end, Betsy outlived her only son born of this brief liaison, who had himself abandoned dreams of royal recognition to marry an ordinary Baltimore heiress. H. L. Mencken, when just married to Goucher professor Sarah Haardt, got a first apartment on Cathedral Street (though he later settled in a house well to the east, near Hollins Market, in an area that has resisted the latest waves of gentrification). He courted Professor Haardt in her apartment at 16 Read Street, his visits chaperoned by a Goucher student who did her homework in the "butler's pantry," as a corner of Professor Haardt's kitchen had formally been designated.

On Biddle Street, a block north of Chase, once lived Gertrude Stein, who wrote:

Pigeons on the grass alas.

Pigeons on the grass alas.

Short longer grass short longer longer shorter yellow grass. Pigeons large pigeons on the shorter longer yellow grass alas pigeons on the grass.

If they were not pigeons what were they.

If they were not pigeons on the grass alas what were they. He had heard of a third and he asked about it it was a magpie in the sky. If a magpie in the sky on the

sky cannot cry if the pigeon on the grass can alas and to
pass the pigeon on the grass alas and the magpie in the
sky on the sky and to try and to try alas on the grass
alas the pigeon on the grass the pigeon on the grass and
alas. They might be very well they might be very well
very well they might be.

  Let Lucy Lily Lily Lucy let Lucy Lucy Lily Lily Lily
Lily let Lily Lucy Lucy let Lily. Let Lucy Lily.

. . . along with many other words and phrases. Stein came
to Baltimore to study medicine at Johns Hopkins University in 1897, one of the few such schools that encouraged women students at that time. Though she left, after
not quite four years, without completing her degree,
Stein did learn to smoke cigars and to box—skills that
must have served her well during her later acquaintance-
ship with Ernest Hemingway.

Also on Biddle Street lived Wallis Warfield Simpson,
not herself a Biddle, though some of her contemporaries
were, such as Elizabeth Gordon Biddle Gordon. When
Edward, Prince of Wales, visited Baltimore in the 1920s,
he professed confusion as to whether he had danced with
a scrapple and had biddle for breakfast or verse vicea,
but he must have enjoyed the dancing more than most
people enjoy eating scrapple,* since he abandoned the

---

*A "savory mush" (Wikipedia) combining flour or cornmeal with hog
offal.

throne of England to become Wallis Warfield Simpson's third husband.

And now Jack and I are leaving Mount Vernon and its elegant ghosts behind. In point of fact, the neighborhood we are leaving is technically called Midtown-Belvedere, and we haven't technically left it yet, quite, but the truly gruesome mock-Tudor row that glowers at us from the north side of Preston Street is a sign that we are nearing some kind of frontier. We are crossing an overpass beneath which the Jones Falls Expressway thunders, faithfully following the course of the buried stream beside it in its S-curve to the north, and from here we have an excellent view of Baltimore's Penn Station. Jack is reminded by the sight that what put the B&O Railroad at a final, fatal disadvantage in its struggle with the Pennsylvania line was the fact that Penn had sole access to the tunnel into New York City. The B&O also provided service into New York, but had to do so by way of a ferry. Thanks in large part to that shortcoming, the equally elegant B&O rail station just a few blocks northwest of where we are now has long been defunct, for travel purposes, and has been taken over by Maryland Institute College of Art, which uses it for exhibition and performance space—and recently the Mount Royal Station has again become a commuter stop, incorporated into the Light Rail route downtown.

Jack looks to the left as we cross Mount Royal Avenue (which curves around past the B&O station into Maryland Institute territory) for a glimpse of "the lovely Lyric

Theater, where I went many times as a child. My mother believed in culture, so I went to a lot of cultural events, and I enjoyed most of them." His favorite act at the Lyric was the "comedian pianist" Victor Borge, a.k.a "the Great Dane," whose unusual blend of music and comedy first became popular in the United States in the forties, thanks to Bing Crosby's radio show. Borge performed into very old age, long enough that Jack was *almost* able to take his daughter Charlotte to see him at the Lyric when she was a small child in the mid 1990s . . . but Borge fell ill at the last minute and canceled the performance, and eventually he died, and Jack and Charlotte saw the Smothers Brothers instead.

We turn into the drive of Penn Station, zigzagging between the heavy concrete barriers that were placed there in 2001 with the idea of making it more difficult for anyone to crash a car bomb into the lobby, and passing through the shadow of a two-story-high, vaguely humanoid sculpture, made out of two colossal sheets of what looks like aluminum, cut out in paper-doll forms and slotted together at right angles, sorta like the wings and fuselage of one of those balsa-wood airplanes you used to get when you were a kid. Well, I don't want to dis this thing, exactly, but I have yet to meet anyone that likes it, and it reminds me of nothing so much as one of those towering tripod military vehicles used by the Martian invaders in *The War of the Worlds*. It materialized sometime in 2004 and has been standing there steadfastly ever since, like a figment of a bad dream that won't go away.

Since Jack often knows that sort of thing, I ask him if he knows exactly how the sculpture got there, but he only shrugs and figures that it was wished on us, like it or not, by some kind of government public art project . . . kind of like the 75 percent gas and electric rate increase that has just been dropped like a bomb on Baltimore, and which has most of the citizenry up in arms. In fact, as I ascertain from subsequent research, the sculpture is called *Male/Female* (one of the paper-doll forms has, um, female secondary sexual characteristics), is the work of Jonathan Borofsky, cost $750,000, and is the result of a "site-specific gift" from the Municipal Arts Society of Baltimore, an organization that has existed since 1899.

We push open the doors to go into the station, another Beaux Arts building, completed in 1911 to replace a brick structure raised on the site in 1885. The elegance of the interior has been very well preserved—it is a pleasant, airy space, with heavy stone columns and lovely stained-glass domes in the entryway, and furnished with heavy wood benches like church pews, most of them empty around noon on a Sunday. We go to the circular information booth in the center of the lobby to snag a MARC schedule for Joy. This train carries commuters between Baltimore and D.C. and, at $14 round-trip, is the best rail travel deal on the East Coast, if not in the whole country.

Schedule in hand, we slip out the side door, back onto Charles, and cross the bridge that spans the tracks. On the far side, at the corner of Lanvale, stands the vast, empty barn of the Chesapeake restaurant, with the same sort of frumpy mock-Tudor trim as adorns Burke's downtown. The Chesapeake was *the* place for seafood up until about 1975, according to Jack, and the fact that nobody has been able to launch any enterprise in the space for the last twenty years or so is generally viewed as a municipal disgrace . . . especially since the rest of the block has lately enjoyed a rebound. A giant **BELIEVE** sign, white letters on a black band, is slathered across the south wall of the vacant restaurant. Believe what, yo?

These signs popped up all over town beginning in the spring 2002, and if you look it up you can discover that they stand for Mayor Martin O'Malley's program to stop, or slow down, drug addiction and the drug trade in Baltimore—a laudable goal, as yet unattained, but I suspect that for most citizens upon whose visual field it intrudes, BELIEVE is no more than a verb without an object.

Should we try believing in a reincarnation of the Chesapeake restaurant? The Charles Theatre, which has been next door to the empty Chesapeake for as long as I can remember, pulled ahead of the Senator as Baltimore's best movie house when it went from a single screen to five. The Charles now hosts the Maryland Film Festival every May, and does a land-office business the rest of the year; for the last several years, there has been a restaurant,

Tapas Teatro, whose side door opens onto the theater's lobby—it's an excellent place, but rather small. Small enough that a restaurant in the Chesapeake space could probably get along pretty well by skimming people out of the line for a table at the tapas place. But no. Or at least not so far.

Across the street from the theater, a wee red neon martini glass is permanently tipping over in the small square window of the Club Charles, casually known to its friends as the Chuck, a venerable hangout for the hip, and ever popular with the *après-théâtre* crowd as well. The Chuck is worth a visit just for its jukebox and its decor; the bar has been piling up recherché objects for decades, and the memorabilia collection has marvelous Art Deco murals for a background. For nonsmokers, and/or non-secondhand smokers, the more recent Café Zodiac next door has similar offerings, plus food; it communicates with the Chuck via the second floor.

Opposite the Club Charles for a spell in the early nineties stood the BAUhouse—brainchild principally of Mark "Mok" Hossfeld, a gentleman who hailed from the South, and was a longtime figure at Louie's bookstore and a presence in the Baltimore underground writing and performance scene. Anarchist and iconoclast, Mok set out to shake things up a bit by bringing big chunks of cultural underground aboveground, into the BAUhouse space, with all predictable seismic shock. It was fun while it lasted, but by '95 or so Mok dematerialized and the BAUhouse along with him—he left behind a Rabelaisian extravaganza of a book called *Doña Juana,* floating in a redolent cloud of mystery. Since then, he's been sighted in Toronto, or in Ganzhou, Jiangxi Province, China, or . . . who knows. Today, there's a crepe shop where the BAUhouse used to be, I think, but I'm not in the mood for crepes right now.

I'm thirsty, now that I think about it, but Club Charles doesn't open till evening, and from there to North Avenue, Charles Street is kinda sorta a dubious area. There are a couple more club-bars that might open later—Club Choices, the Caribbean Paradise Restaurant and Lounge (conveniently nearby to Boot's Bail Bond)—but at this moment, around midday, this stretch has a bit of a derelict feel, and most of the people who are running around yelling, "Yo! Yo!" to get each other's attention seemed to be the worse for something, possibly "substances," possibly just a bad draw from Mother Nature at birth. At the corner, in front of the side wall of Pearson's Florist, there's a woman shuffling along in the bus line, a bandanna wrapped around her head, and the whites of her eyes roll over us as we walk briskly past her, though I have my doubts she's seeing us there, so nodded out on scag does she appear to be.

But Jack remembers a different scene here, back in the sixties, when he would come down to these couple of blocks, which happened to have the only pornography store outside of the Block (not that Jack wasn't comfortable enough on the Block), but the main attraction was music. The local "famous recording artist Ronnie Dove" always had a signboard out somewhere on this strip, informing his public which little club he'd be playing in that night. Here, too, was the Famous Ballroom, home of the Left Bank Jazz Society, which brought in the jazz greats of the sixties for dinner concerts. The Famous Ballroom kitchen kicked out classic southern-fried chicken with grits and greens and biscuits; there "black and white would sit down together," Jack tells me "and listen to Dexter Gordon." Or Cedar Walton or Phil Woods or Art Blakey and the Jazz Messengers—an act that Jack remembers catching when Bobby Watson and Wynton Marsalis were part of the Messengers' configuration.

No more. Baltimore has a hard time supporting a major jazz venue for the last twenty years or so. The club founded by Ethel Waters has changed ownership several times since it was called Ethel's, and though it has always managed to be a good restaurant, the musical offerings are variable. My self-defense trainer and physical therapist, David Shulman, himself a jazz head and amateur musician, sometimes throws together a one-shot concert, in the style of a wildcat house party. But the most durable venue for jazz is the New Haven Lounge, a shotgun bar in a fairly unprepossessing shopping strip in Northwood, east of Loch Raven Boulevard—once you're inside though, the atmosphere changes, helped along by a lot of jazz-scene murals, vaguely in the style of Thomas Hart Benton. A dress code discourages gangsta styling, and while the Haven's clientele is 99 percent black, stray ofays are welcomed kindly, on the assumption that love of the music is shared.

Indeed, I will sometimes go to the Haven for a beer in the late afternoon, well before any live music starts, like, for instance, if I have just come back from Haiti and need a break from looking at white people—it works pretty well so long as I stay away from mirrors, but . . . Anyway, as we cross North Avenue, my head automatically swivels in the direction of the Baltimore Cemetery at its eastern end, till Jack, who's looking the other way, draws my attention to the building that used to house another of Baltimore's covered markets, west along North Avenue, where Jack's mother used to get a lot of her groceries. These markets, strategically distributed all over town, bring a lot of specialized food stores together under one big roof—often in a long building that runs down the center of a street, boulevard style (Hollins Market, Cross Street Market in Federal Hill, the market at the foot of Broadway in Fells Point). Others are housed in big echoing barns, like Lexington Market, still very much a going concern today, which fills up two whole blocks between Eutaw and Greene Streets, just a stone's throw from Edgar Allan Poe's grave. In the days when a cook could have a real *relationship* with a butcher, Jack's mother had her butcher at the North Avenue market, and she had understandings with fishmongers and green-grocers under that roof, too—and it was easy to go there by bus (though she would tote her shopping bags home in a taxi), so it was a blow to her when the market caught fire, and since the North Avenue corridor was beginning to slip downhill then, the market was never rebuilt.

North of North Avenue, the shades of Charles Street grow more bohemian than anything else. "Celebrate Diversity in South Charles Village," exhorts a mural painted on the south facing wall of a building that houses Ebony Style and Dakar African Hair Braiding. Carrying djembe drums and totemic pennants, a handful of Africans and Asians march out of a steely blue cityscape, backed by a flaming red sky. This artwork (so goes its caption) was consummated by thirty-six students from the Maryland Institute College of Art in 1999, and has worn and chipped a good deal since then—most of the other buildings on this block are boarded up. On the next block, things look marginally brighter; we pass an Islamicist Dawah Center, flanked by a halal butcher and the Al Fahr Café, the latter a good bet for spotting local radio personalities on weekdays.

WYPR, the local NPR affiliate, is on the west side of this stretch of Charles, just south of Twenty-fifth Street.

The station used to be called WJHU, but when Johns Hopkins University decided to sell it off to a Chicago-based chain in the early nineties, the station staff, vigorously led by talk-show host Marc Steiner, fought the good fight and raised enough money to take the station independent and give it back to the people of Baltimore. The call letters now stand for Your Public Radio, and people take that seriously.

I bring touring writers onto WYPR shows with some regularity, and the radio staffers have turned me on to various ethnic eateries around the area—there's a string of good Korean restaurants a block west, most notably Nam Kang, and just a few doors east of Charles on Twenty-first Street I notice that Indian Tandoori has its sandwich board out on the sidewalk, which makes me start to salivate like one of Pavlov's unfortunate dogs. Frequented by third-world cabdrivers and WYPR staff and stray cognoscenti from the Hopkins ghetto farther up Charles or the Maryland Institute ghetto southwest below Mount Royal, this place serves a fantabulous buffet, every day but Monday—you can stuff yourself on delicious food for something like seven bucks, and wash it down with mango lassi for about a dollar more. I am tempted, seriously tempted—after all, it is after noon—but Jack would like to make it a little farther before we stop, and on reflection it seems to me that his idea is wiser: After a meal at Indian Tandoori, you waddle a long way before you can walk.

Ornamental fruit trees line these blocks, maybe apples or Bartlett pears. Jack and I have missed their flowering this year. On my first spring visits to Baltimore in the early eighties, I would ride up from the train station (or the bus station maybe) along this avenue of soft white bloom; coming out of the Brooklyn slum I then lived in, it felt like some sort of return to Eden. It's not bad now, though the blossoms have fallen; the trees still provide a grateful shade.

There are hairdressers who purvey the world-famous Baltimore hair extensions, and a couple of thrift shops I used to ransack for skinny ties, and several shops (Wazobia, Sankofa) purveying Afrocentric wares (I used to try to get them to stock Haitian goods). Wazobia is the most venerable of these. The Golden Temple health-food store and lunch counter (originally founded by a couple of Sikhs) disappeared a few years back, though Eckankar, the satsang society that used to provide the Golden Temple with a steady flow of exotically garbed customers, is still functioning, or still has its sign up at least. There's Rita's Lunch, and down in an adjacent basement, Kiyota's Martial Arts Supply, where I was once a regular, back when I went to tae kwon do practice four times a week and wore out my gear more rapidly. I still go once a year for tai chi shoes. You can just barely squeeze your way around the crates of wooden practice swords and body armor and . . . you name it, Kiyota's probably has it somewhere. There's a bulletin board for martial-arts events around town (though some of the notices are illegibly brown), and there is an excellent selection of books (though you may have to shift a few crates to see all of them). It seems to me that Kiyota's is mainly a mail-order outfit, but the store will always find a way to serve a walk-in. Mr. Kiyota, lurking behind the chest-high counter in the back, was a practitioner himself, and may still be; though he has thickened a bit over the years, he still looks very capable. Jack, on the other hand, used to come to these blocks as a kid to pop into a store that no longer exists, Lloyd's Hobby Shop, right across Charles from where Geri's is today, and they'd say to Jack, "Whaddaya want with that glue, kid?" and Jack would protest, "Look at alla models I'm buying!"

If we turned left on Twenty-fifth Street we might just find the Rendezvous Lounge open, on the corner of Howard Street. Called simply the Voo by the late-night crowd, this bar serves aging daytime drinkers up until, oh, 11:00 p.m., at which point a wave of glittering scene makers rolls in from the Maryland Institute, with a sprinkling of Hopkins students from Charles Village. When I and my liver were younger, we used to sit and watch that changing of the guard, and it was better than the circus (probably still is), and free! For the price of a couple of drinks. Also along Twenty-fifth Street west of Charles is what's left of Baltimore's Book Block, the thinking man's answer to the more notorious sex-trade Block on Baltimore Street downtown. Most of the banners commemorating the secondhand book business here vanished when the buildings behind them were torn down to make way for a CVS pharmacy in 1998. Several little bookstores vaporized, their molecules (and much of their stock) redistributed over the Internet. A quasi–cubical lighted sign reading "BOOKS" still hangs in front of Tiber Bookshop, though in the bay window behind a hand-lettered poster referring customers to the American Book Exchange on the Web has faded under the sun to a point very near invisibility.

Next door, Kelmscott Books & Royal Books is still hanging in, which is a whole lot better than nothing. Kelmscott has tunneled through several surviving row houses between its address of record at 32 West Twenty-fifth and the corner of Maryland Avenue and has a huge selection of books on several floors and behind several doors, a lot of them first editions and other collectibles. This specialization protects Kelmscott from undermining by the Book Thing a few blocks northeast, whose generally admirable practice of giving away used books for free has been sort of a poke in the eye for dealers who'd like to make a couple of bucks on them.

We have the willpower not to stop at Kelmscott. Or enough sense not to load ourselves down with books for the good distance we have still to walk. We're passing the offices of the *Afro-American,* founded in Baltimore in 1892 by John Henry Murphy, who had been a slave until 1863. Murphy, who began the paper by consolidating a handful of black church publications, soon made the *Afro-American* the largest-circulation newspaper for black people on the East Coast, instrumental from the earliest days in resisting Jim Crow laws. His five sons, led by Carl Murphy, took over the paper when the founder died in 1922, and brought it to national prominence. Always a spearhead for the civil rights struggle, the *Afro-American* sent its own reporters to Europe and the South Pacific during World War II. Editorially, it campaigned to get more blacks in the Baltimore police and fire departments and in the Maryland state legislature as well. The *Afro-American* was instrumental in ending segregation in the nation's public schools, and fought McCarthyism during the fifties, when Senator Joe's anti-Communist campaigns had targeted Paul Robeson and W. E. B. DuBois, among others. In the 1930s, the paper launched a "Clean Block" program, with the object of making city neighborhoods cleaner and safer; this program still exists today, when the need for it, unfortunately, has not much decreased.

We're in Charles Village now, Lower Charles Village— the closer you get to the Hopkins Homewood campus, the healthier this neighborhood looks, but we are still a few blocks off, and the weeds stand tall in the vacant lots. Here is the back end of the "Old Goucher" neighborhood—the massive Romanesque piles of the original college campus (twenty-two of them all told) front on Saint Paul Street, a block to our east. The centerpiece, Lovely Lane United Methodist Church, had its cornerstone laid in 1884; pastor John Franklin Goucher hired the architect Stanford White to create a monument for the centennial of the Methodist Episcopal Church in the United States. The Women's College of Baltimore grew up around this central bastion of Methodism, and in 1910 changed its name to Goucher College. By the 1940s, the neighborhood had slipped, and indeed had become a red-light district, a situation presumed to be awkward for the young women students, though in the 1980s an elderly alumna was heard to muse, "You know, I learned more looking out my window down there than I ever did in the classroom." Nonetheless, the college removed, in the 1950s, to its present and clearly more pastoral location north of Towson. The Old Goucher neighborhood continued to slide, then turned around in the 1980s, with a major effort to restore the church; the area is now on the National Register of Historic Places.

Meanwhile, Jack and I have paused to gaze upon a really odd couple of buildings standing cheek by jowl to our left. The Baltimore Storage Company—Mayflower is a relatively ordinary six-story stack of red brick, remarkable to me only for my sudden insight that my wife and I stored all our lares and penates here from 1986 to 1988, when we were on an extended walkabout elsewhere, and jeez, I never looked at the building before! The building next to it is more visually interesting, perplexing even: Its windowless front seems to be covered with a skin of metal panels, tilted at slight angles this way and that—like the tiles on the space shuttle, maybe? On closer inspection, these panels all turn out to be cement, their metallic appearance produced by silver paint—a space-age rejoinder to Formstone, one might say. Jack remembers this structure was built to house a radio station and sound studio—the metallic facade was intended to express the state-of-the-artness (circa 1965) of all the gizmology within.

Looking at the Mayflower emblem seems to put Jack in mind of the fact that the duck canvas sailcloth for clipper ships and other such vessels used to be manufactured in this area. Appalachian immigrants who populated Hampden, the neighborhood on the west side of the Hopkins Homewood campus from where we're standing, began to spill over into Lower Charles Village during World War II, just as the sailcloth industry fizzled out for good, leaving packs of the newcomers unemployed. But what really killed the stately north-south streets like Charles was cars, Jack says; a neighborhood can only tolerate so much traffic before civilized life is eroded.

For that the city can thank, or blame, traffic engineer Henry Barnes, who soon after World War II made several of Baltimore's longest north-south streets (Charles, Maryland, Calvert, Saint Paul) one way, fitting them out with staggered signals that permit automobiles extremely long, uninterrupted runs. The calm boulevards of all the neighborhoods we've just been walking through were thus turned into high-speed corridors, or in the words of a 1991 *New Yorker* article, "mini-expressways." We want to be careful how we whine about this result, given Baltimore's shortage of full-scale expressways. One of my favorite semisecrets of local locomotion is that between 5:00 and 6:30 p.m., when the rest of the town is caught in the most contorted cloaca of rush hour, I can gun through timed traffic lights up one-way Calvert Street from Harborplace to Northern Parkway in ten or twelve minutes—home by fifteen. But I don't see much along the way. Pedestrian traffic—leisurely strollers and local shoppers—is downright discouraged by the rocket tubes that the north-south streets have turned into.

Charles Street is one way north, which is, of course, the way we're going, and though the day has waxed into afternoon during the course of our promenade, we aren't exactly getting blown off the sidewalk by cars shooting by. As we get closer to the Hopkins campus, there is in fact more foot traffic. At Twenty-seventh Street, we stop a minute to admire a gray stone building with a keeplike structure rounding the northwest corner. The Johns Hopkins University Press is now domiciled there, but back in the sixties it was the first place Jack moved into on his own. "It's nice to have someone in the family living on Charles Street again!" his mother cheerfully remarked at the time, blissfully unaware of the extent to which the building was a hippie drug den in those days.

To our left, Charles Street has become a boulevard—
the northbound corridor uneasily balanced by a solitary
lane that creeps south from University Parkway as far as
Twenty-ninth Street, where it disappears. Beyond the
trees, the basin of Wyman Park falls away from the west
side of Charles Street, then rises again toward the facade
of the Baltimore Museum of Art (BMA). This sweet little bowl of a park is popular with dog walkers and tod-
dlers with their minders by day. After dark, it draws
stargazers and the odd pot smoker, and once in a while a
gay prostitution scandal flares up. Wyman Park Drive
wraps around the southern edge of the park, then
(changing its name to San Martin near the Homeland
campus's southern gate) squiggles through a narrow strip
of woods along the western edge of campus, through a
series of very tight hairpin turns as far as University Parkway. Before Hopkins expanded to the western side of it,
this stretch of San Martin used to be a good place to
practice mountain driving . . . but now there are too
many speed bumps, campus police, and woolgathering
professors for the exercise to be properly relaxing.

To our left, as we cross Thirty-first Street, is the
quaint little office of the *Johns Hopkins News-Letter,* a
very small building perched astride a gulley, as if it had
been expanded (ever so slightly) from a springhouse.
Adjacent are the outdoor sculpture gardens of the Baltimore Museum of Art, with a pleasant walkway wending
through them into the campus. The upper tier of the

sculpture garden doubles as a dining patio for Gertrude's, the excellent restaurant housed in the museum. The BMA's collections rival those of the Walters downtown. The great jewel there is the collection of Claribel and Etta Cone; Claribel, who did become a doctor, was friendly with Gertrude Stein at the Johns Hopkins medical school, and thanks to this friendship she bought in early on Picasso and Matisse (whom they visited in their Paris studios). The collection also includes a wealth of paintings by Renoir, Gauguin, Cézanne, and many others: a thick slice straight from the foundation period of early twentieth-century modern art.

On our right hand, we are leaving behind what Jack designates as "the horrible Catholic church I had to go to as a kid," known to the general public as Saints Philip and James. The heavyweight domed building looks magnificent from the outside, but as a child Jack found the interior "dark and scary," and he has especially unfond memories of an Irish monsignor there—the opposite, as black is to white, of the twinkling jovial Irish priests you see in the movies. "If you went to confession to him, you felt terrible on the way in and even worse on the way out," Jack reminisces, without much nostalgia, really. Catholicism was a strong constant in his peripatetic childhood, and he graduated from Loyola High School (at the far north end of Charles Street) in 1967, but in retrospect he doesn't see it as a positive influence: "If you have the wrong kind of psychology"—as I reckon Jack reckons he does—"being a Catholic is bad for you."

Like it or not, Jack lived close enough to walk to Saints Philip and James for most of his childhood. Indeed, for a short time, he and his mother lived behind the green awning we are passing just now, while waiting for another apartment to open, at 2905 North Charles— a building as close to the church as its rectory.

To our left, the Hopkins campus unfolds. The university has been doing a lot of construction since I taught there, in the large undergraduate division of the Writing Seminars, in the 1990s. The campus is rather small, and in those days JHU only had dorm rooms enough for its freshman and sophomore population. Upperclasspersons were flung upon central Charles Village, east of Charles Street. Sent out into something similar to the real world so early, the Hopkins undergrads matured sooner, in certain practical respects, than their peers in other more sheltered schools who spend all four years in the hive. I'm not sure what the housing situation is now, but Hopkins has opened a capacious student center fronting on Charles, with fifty-three thousand square feet of media centers, art and dance studios, and other such amenities. Hopkins is one of the few universities in the United States to have been designed on the German model: The research undertaken by the full-time faculty is the first priority, and the graduate students come second. The entire undergraduate program was added on well after these other elements of the university were firmly in place. If the care and feeding of Hopkins undergraduates often seems to be addressed by afterthought, the Mattin Center is a rather nice afterthought, after all.

There are some recently added shops and restaurants on the east side of Charles—for example, a Ruby Tuesday and a couple of fancy new coffee shops—but Jack and I pass on all of these and turn right on Thirty-second Street, just south of the splendid Mattin Center, intending to eat at Niwana, a pleasant Asian-fusion restaurant we both know quite well (it is, to be sure, owned and operated by Baltimore Koreans). But Niwana is closed, we hope not for keeps—the east end of the block, at the corner of Saint Paul Street, seems to have taken a few hard blows from a wrecking ball.

"Struever Bros. Eccles and Rouse" is writ large all over the construction equipment, which, on Sunday, stands idle on the blocks of Saint Paul south of Thirty-third Street. The company has three monster projects in this area. Village Lofts, a condo complex that looks mostly finished from the outside, fills the whole east side of Saint Paul between Thirty-second and Thirty-first Streets. Across the street, Charles Commons will add 618 beds of student housing (and a good thing, too, for rents in Charles Village are apt to rise sharply when all of this condo universe is completed) and have the Hopkins Barnes & Noble bookstore on the ground floor, in much more spacious quarters than it occupies now, in the basement of a classroom building on campus. The Olmsted, an equally vast retail and condo combo featuring among other things a five-hundred-plus-car garage, is slated to go up on the west side of Saint Paul between Thirtysecond and Thirty-third. I can't figure out if I think Frederick Law Olmsted and his city-planning descendants would be pleased to have the family name on this colossus or not, but Jack, anyway, does not see Struever Bros. as *apostles of evil*—on the contrary, he thinks they've done great work in revitalizing areas all around town. The name is properly pronounced "Streever," rather than the more intuitive "Stroover," I learn as we pick our way south over rubble and around barricades. Jack became friends with Bill Struever in the 1970s "after he had come here with Cobber Eccles, his brother Fred, and some other people, I think from Brown. I was going out with a girl who got a job at his company. It was very exciting to watch them redevelop South Baltimore and the Cross Street Market" (the latter yet another of Baltimore's covered markets, not far from the Lippman-Simon enclave in Federal Hill).

Meanwhile, the old commercial block on the east side of Saint Paul between Thirty-first and Thirty-second is more or less the same as it used to be. The little grocery store and the small liquor store with the great collection of weird old decanters are still there. On the south corner, the old pharmacy with the merchandise dating back to the fifties has been replaced by the spiffier Donna's restaurant, all done up in black and industrial metallic. The Homewood Deli, whose attendants never quailed at making you a corned beef, coleslaw, and chopped liver sandwich (better than it sounds!) has been gone for several years. In its place is the sort of "neighborhood bar" that thinks of itself in quotation marks and probably got its idea of itself from the TV show *Cheers*.

We're going somewhere considerably more old school: the Charles Village Pub, which has been on this spot for considerably longer than I've been in Baltimore, anyway. It's a pleasant, subaqueous dim green shade inside. The bar runs along the south wall, and opposite there's a line of booths beneath a wide area of black-and-white photos of heroes of any and all sports ever played in Baltimore, all of them soundly laminated into place by a couple of generations worth of cigarette smoke and vaporized fry oil. It's somewhere between noon and one, and the bar is about half full of torpid-looking college-age kids, slowly backing out of their Sunday hangovers with the help of one or two hairs of the dog.

Jack and I slide into a booth. We order burgers with fried onions on them, not feeling too guilty about that for once, given the number of miles we've walked. And have still to walk, for that matter. While we wait for our burgers, and then while we are eating them, too, Jack tells me more about his father's military days. The recent film *Good Night, and Good Luck* has put him in mind of the McCarthy era, and he particularly admires how the movie manages to convict Senator Joe out of his own mouth, simply by running old news footage of his most appalling public statements.

Jack's father, it turns out, was a peripheral victim of the McCarthyite witch hunt, and, of course, as he points out to me through his clenched teeth (with, so far, no burger between them), we'll never know how many hundreds or thousands such unknown victims there may have been, since the McCarthyite technique was mainly based on secret, anonymous blackballing. John Henry Heyrman had the ill luck to be stationed at Camp Kilmer and Fort Dix during the period that McCarthy was "investigating" a phantom Communist spy ring at Fort Monmouth, a third military base in New Jersey. No actual spy was ever discovered, and the titanic battle between McCarthy and the military ended with Senator Joe's disgrace and departure from national politics. In the meantime, though, some McCarthy acolyte slipped a damning letter into John Henry Heyrman's file, a deft web of innuendo that did its considerable best to taint every phase of his military career, from the beginning, with a shade of Commie red. Heyrman was never stationed at Fort Monmouth, but apparently serving in the military anywhere in New Jersey was enough to draw him a McCarthyite dagger in the back. Not until several years later, when he was stationed in Korea, did he find out about this poison-pen document, thanks to a friend in the Pentagon who tipped Jack off about it. Jack's father needed several years of effort, and a bale of paperwork, to get the libelous letter expunged from his record. By then he'd long since abandoned the military to seek his fortune elsewhere.

A bit dazed by this tale, I follow Jack out onto Saint Paul, blinking in the afternoon sunlight that spills very generously down the street. Between Thirty-second and Thirty-third, the block of modest row houses on the east side of Saint Paul is in the early stages of demolition. Trees in the comically tiny front yards have been uprooted and shoved by dozer blades up toward the equally tiny white frame porches. Struever, Eccles, et cetera have sealed the whole row off with storm fence till they can get around to destroying the rest of it. When I first moved to Baltimore, I lived on a very similar block in the Hampden-Remington area, on the far side of the Hopkins campus from where we are now. These were pleasant, unpretentious two-story homes, attractive enough and quite comfortable inside, though I admit they had certain drawbacks—for example, if any one house on the row had rats, they found it easy to build their own rodent railroads through all the shared attic and basement walls. Rented for decades to a transient student population, this block of Saint Paul probably has worse problems of that ilk, and yet I do feel sorta sad to see it go.

As we have been eating onions, we pop into Wawa on the corner of Thirty-third Street to purchase some breath mints. This store has been on this location for so long that members of the adjacent Sigma Alpha Epsilon fraternity are more commonly called "Wawa brothers." The store has an international flavor now, as much as a convenience store can. While Jack scores the mints, I stand back and admire: Where an ordinary mom-'n'-pop operation might display the first greenback it ever earned, a display of maybe 150 banknotes from different nations all over the planet covers a four-foot square above the registers—and I wonder if somebody tried to pass all of them here?

Whistling with our new minty breath, we walk back over to Charles Street. Opposite Thirty-third Street's dead end, students at semester's end are basking on the wide sloping greensward in front of the library, known among them as "the Beach." At the north end of that tilted circle of grass stands Homewood House, which Charles Carroll gave his son $10,000 to build—a stupendous sum in 1800, when the gift was made. The junior Carroll soon quarreled with his father over cost overruns that brought the total price tag to a whopping forty K, but the result, a lovely airy structure built on a symmetrical Palladian design, is one of Baltimore's brightest jewels of Federal architecture. Homewood House was a genuine country retreat when the Carrolls built it, standing in the midst of a 130-acre farm, a world away from downtown Baltimore. But the city grew out to embrace it, and Johns Hopkins University (whose campus takes the name as well as the territory of the nineteenth-century Carroll estate) restored the building, equipped with period furniture and decorations and now operates it as a museum.

Jack's Auntie May, "a wild spinster woman," used to live in an apartment house called simply "The Charles," opposite the Hopkins Beach, while his grandmother lived a few blocks northwest, at 100 University Parkway . . . although few of her correspondents bothered with such finicking details of her address, for letters addressed only to

Mrs. F. C. Latrobe
Baltimore, Maryland

reached her unfailingly. As a boy, Jack often had the duty of escorting his grandmother to visit Auntie May. Mrs. F. C. Latrobe was then on crutches and getting her in and out of the requisite taxicabs always involved some perturbation. The visits could be volatile, too, since Auntie May usually managed to exasperate the older woman with her wild, spinsterish ways. When I try quizzing Jack for details of wild spinsterism (well, perhaps I oughtn't to be so interested), he claims to have been too young to remember—only seven or eight at the time of these encounters.

A nice thing about growing up in this area was free run of the Hopkins campus and the surrounding area, which was much less built up then than it is now. Hopkins is not the sort of institution to operate and maintain a football team. Lacrosse substitutes as the obsessional sport, not only at Hopkins but practically everywhere else in Baltimore, from middle school on up. The lacrosse stadium—now a well-enclosed structure on the southwest corner of Charles and University Parkway, which we have just turned onto—was an open field when Jack was a kid, and going to the games was free. Across University Parkway, the neighborhood kids had a dirt-lot baseball diamond where the Colonnade, a fashionable hotel-cum-condo, stands now. Its restaurant, Four West, is popular with the Hopkins crowd, and people like to duck in to see the cunning trompe l'oeil painting on the ceiling of the lobby.

Where other high-rise apartment buildings run northwest along the diagonal of University Parkway, there used to be just a handful of mansions, spreading east from Roland Park, set on vast lots whose expansiveness now provides parking for the higher-density housing now in place. We're wending our way through all that now, walking north on Canterbury Road, slipping into what's officially called Tuscany-Canterbury—one of those odd little secluded neighborhoods you're not likely to know about if you don't live there or know someone who does. These are pleasant, secluded, tree-lined streets, with mostly modest houses, and a few grander ones. Better-off Hopkins faculty live in here, and they can walk to work. To our east along Thirty-ninth Street is Cloverhill Road, though it seems a bit much to call it a road, since it is only one block long. On its one block was the most settled residence of Jack's childhood.

Continuing on Canterbury across Thirty-ninth Street, we stop for a moment in front of No. 3923, a pleasant, smallish two-story brick with a bay window trimmed in white—where Jack's mother spent *her* childhood. "She didn't stray far," Jack says after a minute. "Just all over the world." Curiously, her father, F. C. Latrobe Jr., son of the mayor, never owned a house of his own but always rented.

Canterbury Road makes a T stop at West Highfield, behind the caramel stone pile of a house that has been for many years the home and headquarters of John Waters. Jack's grandparents used to go to dinner there, because they knew the architect who built it, and I have been to dinner there thanks to an amiable acquaintance with John Waters, who is a great cook, among his many other talents. I have seen his collection of art by serial killers, and his needlepoint seat covers of Baltimore scenes, so it seems a little sneaky to go creeping along past the rear of the house, mostly sheltered by a stand of bamboo, without so much as a by-your-leave—but Jack assures me that this trail is in fact a public right of way, and has been since time immemorial.

There's a little stone bridge at a dip in a trail, and under it runs water from a spring somewhere to the east, hidden in the bamboo, and to the west the water becomes a little creek maybe six feet wide. Jack hops down and picks his way over the boulders that line the streambed for twenty yards or so, gazing toward the point it disappears into a culvert. He and other boys used to dare each other to crawl all the way through that pipe to where it emerges at Linkwood Road, quite a considerable distance on the other side of the Calvert School campus, at whose eastern edge the culvert begins—he doesn't say if anybody ever did it, though, and I sure don't feel like trying it now. At Linkwood, this rivulet flows into Stony Run on its way south to join the Jones Falls, and a hiking trail along Stony Run (part of the Olmsteds' 1904 park plan for Baltimore), using bits of an old Maryland and Pennsylvania railroad right of way north to Roland Park and south through the windings of Wyman Park to a point just a hair north of the woods of Druid Hill. At that point the Jones Falls Expressway forms a more serious barrier to the hiker than the Jones Falls stream probably used to do, though there is a plan to link the Stony Run trail to a ten-mile footpath along the Jones Falls streambed.

But we are going another way, cutting across a corner of the Calvert School campus. Calvert, world famous for its correspondence courses, also does very well by Balti-more day students in grades one through eight. We huff up one of Calvert's driveways and rejoin Charles at a sharp bend at the intersection of Warrenton Road, where the curve is outlined with a metal rail and a row of bright yellow and black arrows, humming like bumble-bees, to let drivers know that "THE ROAD TURNS HERE." Judging from the dings on the rail, a fair num-ber of drivers don't process the message in time.

And on we go, headed north toward Cold Spring Lane, a street constructed in 1806 to improve access to today's Roland Park. Down in a declivity to our left, in a pocket enclosed by a loop of Whitfield Road, is a curi-ous oval track, suitable for skateboard or miniature pony races; it's the sort of thing you don't see unless you are on foot, so neither of us has ever seen it before, and neither of us can explain it.

At Cold Spring, we stop to wait for the light, con-templating a three-foot-high sculpture of a Maryland blue crab, dressed in a cap and gown to commemorate its placement at the corner of the Loyola College campus here. The crabs are a sequel to a 2001 "Fish out of Water" project, in which fish sculptures of a similar size were decorated by various local artists in a manner evok-ing the sites where they were placed. I thought the fish were pretty cool, but the crabs seem . . . overly predeter-mined by comparison; the fish offer more blank canvas to the creative mind and hand. Born in the Creative Alliance, the Crabtown project has posted some two hundred statuesque crustaceans around town, some more cunningly decorated than others.

What Jack thinks of this particular crab I don't find out, because the light turns green and we mush on. To our west, Cold Spring drops into a dip where the Stony Run trail cuts through on its way south, and in the couple of commercial blocks where the street rises are a couple of beloved Baltimore institutions: the most eclectic video store, Video Americain, and what's left of Alonso's, which is about half of it. Alonso's was once a true-classic neighborhood bar, with a tiny liquor and convenience store in the front and no natural light source in the long back room, which was mostly filled by the huge black oval bar—you could just squeak around the edges of the room—and decorated with curiosities like a 3-D topographical map of the Battle of the Little Bighorn, which I sorely wish I had tried to buy when the place was sold up a few years back. A team of middle-aged waitresses of the Hon variety worked inside the oval counter. They had sizable hair and wore white shirts and black vests and little black bow ties; most of them chain-smoked, and did frequently call you "Hon." Facing the sidewalk was the smallest display window I have ever seen, a twelve-inch-square chest high in the Formstone wall, containing a well-aged jug of clear eau-de-vie with a whole pear inside. I figure the owners probably drank it when they sold the place. Anyway, I hope they did.

Alonso's was famous then for their one-pound hamburger, and still are. They now also offer a pound-and-a-half hamburger, which I consider to be de trop. Try to get a hamburger less than sixteen ounces there—they don't serve one. The new management cut the oval bar in half and stuck it into the east wall, which is the kind of thing that makes me want to cry. I don't know what they did with the other half. The new management doesn't allow smoking in the place, so the chain-smoking waitresses went elsewhere. In Maryland, it's illegal to smoke in *restaurants,* but *bars,* with the recent exception of Alonso's, are still blue with tobacco fumes, so I figure the chain-smoking waitresses wouldn't have had too hard a time finding congenial work. The no-smoking policy means I can now take my family to Alonso's, which is still a nice place. The hamburgers are still good, and the old bar now communicates through the east wall with Loco Hombre, which started as a sort of burrito barn, then briefly (and pleasantly) morphed into a subdued expensive gourmet Mexican restaurant that the neighborhood couldn't quite support. Finally, Loco Hombre decided to accept and embrace its identity crisis, and now they serve a little bit of everything, and most of it's pretty good. They have great margaritas, five different kinds.

The old Alonso's used to draw from the apartment houses east on Cold Spring, which had a lot of retirees in them up till the early nineties, when Loyola began to transform itself from a sleepy little Catholic college whose students were mostly commuters to a dynamic small liberal arts college that draws a lot of students from out of town and out of state. As we walk north on the east side of Charles, I am speculating out loud about how the old folks must have been kinda dismayed when they found that their building had turned into a boisterous college dorm, and Jack agrees and smiles and shrugs and says, briefly, "Progress is cruel." I think about that for a minute and realize that in spite of or along with his great knowledge and deep fondness for Baltimore history, Jack is actually a very progressive sort of guy, which probably explains why his attachment to the Latrobe lineage is limited, and also why he suffers fools and foolishness most miserably.

The sidewalk ends at a point where Loyola has constructed a two-story-high pedestrian bridge to enable its students to get across the Charles Street corridor without being run over. We stare up at that for a minute and then decide that we might do as well to cut across a couple of lawns to a point where the sidewalk resumes. It has been a remarkably cool and breezy May day for Baltimore, where spring usually segues into sweltering summer heat in about fifteen minutes and stays that way until October, but now at two or three in the afternoon the sun is high and it's pretty hot and we have been walking quite a long way, most of it uphill, as Joy pointed out when we planned the excursion. Why not walk *down* Charles Street? Joy had asked, but Jack pointed out that downhill or not, that would be upstream in the historical sense, and I agreed with him.

Gratefully, we come into some shade. There is a wide swath of woods on the east side of Charles here, and Blythewood Road sweeps through it, lined with lovely secluded houses in the wooded dell and on the ridge overlooking Stony Run. This small and distinctly exclusive neighborhood gets its name from Evergreen House on the west side of Charles, built in 1857 by the Broadbent family. Twenty-one years later the house was purchased by a B&O Railroad magnate, John Work Garrett, as a gift to his son, T. Harrison Garrett, who went on improving the grounds and expanding the house, as did their son, who was named for his Garrett grandfather. The senior John Work Garrett had piloted the B&O Railroad through the Civil War, furnishing coal to the White House and making sure the trains ran on time for Union troops. His fortune was made, in large part, by the colossal transshipment facility he created in Locust Point, but he was also notorious for paying his workers more stingily than any other railroad did.

The Garretts were art collectors on the level of the Cone sisters or the Walters family, and the Johns Hopkins University now operates the forty-eight-room house as a museum, featuring a marvelous rare-book library and a fantastic collection of netsukes, among many, many other items—more than fifty thousand all told. I am a fancier of netsukes in particular, but Evergreen House is high on a hill and neither Jack nor I am disposed to climb it right now. As we pass by, Jack looks up the hill and recalls that John H. B. Latrobe was the first lawyer for the B&O Railroad—it was in that capacity that he began amassing the huge fortune that later generations spent their way through.

Evergreen House is tucked into place by the calm green campus of the College of Notre Dame of Maryland on its north side; in the old order of things, Notre Dame used to be the sister school to Loyola. In the old order of things, the Boumi Temple used to stand here on the west side of Charles, at the corner of Wyndhurst. A big stone edifice in a sort of pseudo-Egyptian style, it stood at the head of a curving drive on top of a little colline, with a long swoop of lawn falling down to the roadway from it, calm and silent as a mausoleum. Empty, too. The Boumi Temple was a Masonic building, so no one else ever went into it, and the Masons seemed to use it no more than once a year, so the Boumi Temple really didn't do anything, it just *was.*

This much it accomplished in a stately manner. Then Loyola bought the property, slaughtered the building, and put up an enormous gym right flush with the roadway, alongside which we are passing. There are lots of plateglass windows on the street side, so normally, when school is in, you see the students being flogged and flung about across an acre of high-tech exercise equipment inside. But now school is out and the interior of the gym seems to be deserted, though there have been a few joggers coming past us on the sidewalk. Pretty girls, some of them. Progress is cruel. I grumble a bit about the loss of the Boumi Temple, which though one could hardly have called it functional did manage to beautify the corner where it stood. Jack nods and then reflects, aloud, that the greatest threat to Roland Park is that developers should get their claws into Saint Mary's Seminary, which occupies a still-more-monumental piece of real estate to our west, at the corner of Northern Parkway and Roland Avenue, on the slope above the Jones Falls. Though never so vacant as Masonic lodges, Catholic seminaries have tended to be depopulated of late.

Jack's thought is an unpleasant one, and I push it out of my mind as we pause at the top of the rise beyond Wyndhurst. In the dip beyond is Friends School, which Jack and Joy's fifteen-year-old daughter has attended since first grade; there, too, is the Baltimore Friends Meeting House, a modest stone building standing in a grove of trees just past the school, and then, on the next upward roll of ground, the colossal twin towers of the Cathedral of Mary Our Queen. A co-cathedral with Benjamin Latrobe's basilica downtown, it was completed in 1959, on a plan roughly similar to Notre Dame in Paris, though with less in the way of Gothic elaboration of the details. The Baltimore cathedral's lines are more severe and indeed quite elegant. A bequest from the

O'Neill who owned the downtown department store paid for its construction. Whenever there's a major Catholic funeral here (Johnny Unitas, not long ago, and a policeman killed in the line of duty are the two that come to my mind at the moment), the cathedral towers are circled by news and traffic helicopters, whose wide ellipse carries them over my house on Pinehurst Road.

We don't go that way, but instead take a detour, east across Charles onto Saint Albans, which soon takes a very sharp bend to the north, passing through the northwest end of Homeland. The sight of the cathedral has put Jack's mind on Catholicism again, and he is telling me that by the time Charles Carroll was in his prime, on the eve of the American Revolution, it was illegal to be a Catholic in Maryland, whose founder had meant it for a Catholic sanctuary. Carroll practiced his religion clandestinely, which is why he needed Benjamin Latrobe to build him a private chapel at his estate in Carrollton.

Charlotte walks home from school most days, weather permitting, and recently she took Jack on a tour of her route, which she has carefully researched and developed toward the goal of Shortest Possible Distance. Her pathway takes her through various Homeland alleys, a feature that alarmed Jack for her safety, as he tells me now. I propose that Homeland alleys aren't really very dangerous. At least not by day, and probably not ever. In fact, they are almost as carefully kept up as the streets and sidewalks and front lawns of Homeland, so that the most shocking thing a pedestrian would be apt to encounter would be maybe a dent in somebody's trash can; moreover, there are usually people at home in these houses during the daytime, I suggest, looking out their kitchen windows as Charlotte lopes by . . . And Jack seems to find these arguments reasonably persuasive.

Our risk, meanwhile, is getting run over while we cross four lanes of Northern Parkway at Saint Albans, which doesn't have a traffic light, but we don't. There is noticeably less spring in my step than there was when we started, but we make it across without mishap, and head east into Cedarcroft on Melrose, passing a retirement home enigmatically entitled the Long Green, in fact a long, white, two-story barn, which looks peaceful enough, and where I have never seen the faintest sign of human activity. East of this establishment is a gracious little run downhill to Pinehurst Road. Getting my breath, I take a squint at Jack as we go down. Jack has black hair and a black beard and something of a black bear's bulk, or so I remember, but all of a sudden he looks slimmer. Has he lost ten pounds since we started walking? I wish I thought I had, but I don't.

I pass a remark on how fit he seems, and he agrees and said he's been working at it, getting up early enough to play a couple of sets of tennis with Joy before setting out for Clean Cuts, be it in Washington or Hampden. His Latrobe forebears, he tells me, all had the basic appearance of the tycoon caricature on the Monopoly game box. They also tended to die of heart failure, on the early side. Therefore Jack has taken some pains to shed the ancestral profile.

By this time, we have reached the corner of Lake and Pinehurst, which is where we part. We are each a block from home, but in different directions from this point. Jack pulls out a cell phone, somewhat to my surprise—one of those flat square ones with a tiny keyboard on the front—and begins punching buttons and looking at the screen. I ask him if he wants to call us a cab, and we both laugh, but not very loud.

Beale-ti-More Or?

*I*RELAND'S BEALE-TI-MORE, WHERE GEORGE CAL-vert picked up the name and noble title, is found in County Cork, toward the southwest coastline where Erin's green shore begins to fray into the North Atlantic. Some in Ireland referred to it as the parish closest to America. A Celt named Lug 11 founded the place. Vikings invaded it in the ninth century. In 1631, just five years after the Calverts had become lords of this lonely manor, County Cork's Baltimore was raided by Algerian pirates, who left their names on some of the pubs. The O'Driscoll clan, descendants of the original Lug 11 who ruled the Irish Baltimore until the Calverts came, had (like many of the finest old families everywhere in the world) been pirates themselves back in the day. The Calverts's tenure there was brief, and the O'Driscolls had their Irish Baltimore fief restored to them by Charles II in 1660.

Before the O'Driscolls, the Druids were there, or maybe the O'Driscolls were Druids themselves, up to a point. The O'Driscolls built a castle on the hill that the Druids had named Dún na Séad, meaning "Hill of Jewels," and politely called it "Castle Dun Na Sead." Beale-ti-more, from which Baltimore is roughly corrupted, is usually thought to mean "Town of the Big House," but a better translation is "Great Habitation of Bel"—the Celtic deity of light, worshipped among others by Hammurabi, the law-giving Babylonian king, and by the Druids here, descendants of Lug. A Franciscan friary was built in the area in 1460, following the universal practice of building temples of new religions in the precincts of the old sanctuaries—so that the energy of the old practices is absorbed into the new ones, and the memory of the old ways is diffused and erased.

THE AMERICAN INDIANS who lived where Baltimore stands now have left very little evidence of who they were or what they were like. The word *Patapsco*, or "backwater," is almost the strongest trace of them. Scattered and constantly moving around the Chesapeake Bay area were Algonquian-speaking tribes: the Anacostians, Piscataways, Matawomans, Nanjemoys, Potpocos, Chapticos, Pawtuxents (they named a river), Nanticokes, and Tockwoghs, to mention only a few. From the north, there had begun to arrive Iroquoian-speaking tribes: the

Susquehannocks, Massawomecks, and Tuscarora. With these new arrivals came war. There were also raids into the Chesapeake Bay area by Virginia Indians called Minqua or Mingo.

Indians lived near the water in woven houses, sometimes surrounded by stockades. They hunted and gathered and fished and planted a little corn. They left behind arrowheads and remnants of baskets and pottery and heaps of empty clam and oyster shells for the curious colonists to peruse. An early arrival, Father Andrew White, described the indigenous people he met: " . . . very tall and well proportioned; their skin is naturally rather dark . . . they generally have black hair, which they carry round in a knot to the left ear, and fasten with a band, adding some ornament . . . they are clothed for the most part in deerskins or some similar kind of clothing which hangs down behind like a cloak. They wear aprons round the middle and leave the rest of the body naked."

But by the time the Europeans swarmed in, American Indians had already mostly disappeared from the Patapsco River valley. War parties of Seneca used the Baltimore area as a trail for attacking the Piscataways. There are still some Piscataways in Prince George's County, mostly absorbed into the European-American population now, thanks to generations of intermarriage, and thus diluted, dissipated, disappeared . . . There is a Baltimore American Indian Center, on Broadway in Fells Point, that helps Native Americans from all over adjust to new communities. Every summer they put on a powwow in Patterson Park. But they don't seem to feature much in the way of direct descendants of the tribes who used to live here.

PROGRESS IS CRUEL. In their need to survive and establish themselves, new cultures devour the old ones, one way or another. Sometimes the new cultures deal with the old ones by full-on assault—as with Christians and heathens the world over (or, if you prefer, as with Muslims and infidels). Sometimes the consumption, the digestion, of the old by the new is accomplished slowly, delicately, imperceptibly, through a leisurely osmosis, until one day you look around and see that your world has been unrecognizably transformed.

Three or four hundred years ago, the roads I've walked with my friends in Baltimore were bison trails, "bear-brakes" (in Mrs. Trollope's felicitous phrase), or maybe just trackless, virgin forest. And far out on the edge of some glade or cliff or stream stood a person or two with nothing at all in common with me but the simple fact of humanity. I would have liked to see them, too. At least, I think I would.

Acknowledgments

For the history of Baltimore's streets, I often relied on *Walking in Baltimore: An Intimate Guide to the Old City,* by Frank R. Shivers Jr. *Streetwise Baltimore: The Stories Behind Baltimore Street Names,* by Carleton Jones, delivered just what its title promises. I found a wealth of anecdotes in two delicious collections of *Baltimore Sun* columns by Rafael Alvarez: *Hometown Boy: The Hoodle Patrol and Other Curiosities of Baltimore* and *Storyteller;* anyone who likes this book should go on to those two.

I would like to thank my feet for staying under me during these rambles. For all the others who helped me on the way, more than likely you will find your names in these pages, and thank you kindly for all you did.

About the Author

MADISON SMARTT BELL is the author of twelve novels, including *The Washington Square Ensemble* (1983), *Waiting for the End of the World* (1985), *Straight Cut* (1986), *The Year of Silence* (1987), *Doctor Sleep* (1991), *Save Me, Joe Louis* (1993), *Ten Indians* (1997), and *Soldier's Joy*, which received the Lillian Smith Award in 1989. Bell has also published two collections of short stories: *Zero db* (1987) and *Barking Man* (1990). In 2002, the novel *Doctor Sleep* was adapted as a film—*Close Your Eyes*, starring Goran Visnjic, Paddy Considine, and Shirley Henderson. *Forty Words for Fear*, an album of songs cowritten by Bell and Wyn Cooper and inspired by the novel *Anything Goes*, was released by Gaff Music in 2003; other performers include Don Dixon, Jim Brock, Mitch Easter, and Chris Frank.

Bell's eighth novel, *All Souls' Rising*, was a finalist for the 1995 National Bank Award and the 1996 PEN/Faulkner Award, and winner of the 1996 Anisfield-Wolf

Award for the Best Book of the Year, dealing with matters of race. *All Souls' Rising,* along with the second and third novels of his Haitian Revolutionary trilogy, *Master of the Crossroads* and *The Stone That the Builder Refused,* is available in a uniform edition from Vintage Contemporaries. *Toussaint Louverture: A Biography* appeared from Pantheon in 2007.

Born and raised in Tennessee, he has lived in New York and in London and now lives in Baltimore, Maryland. A graduate of Princeton University (B.A. 1979) and Hollins College (M.A. 1981), he has taught in various creative writing programs, including the Iowa Writers' Workshop and the Johns Hopkins University Writing Seminars. Since 1984, he has taught at Goucher College, along with his wife, the poet Elizabeth Spires. He is currently director of the Kratz Center for Creative Writing at Goucher College and has been a member of the Fellowship of Southern Writers since 2003. For more details, visit http://faculty.goucher.edu/mbell.

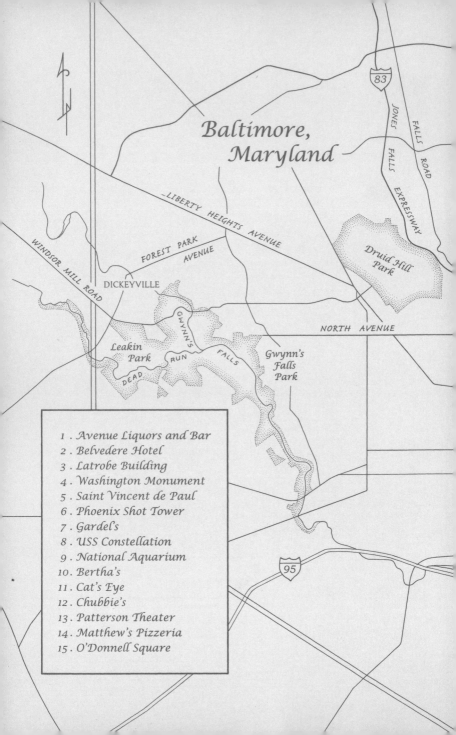

Baltimore, Maryland

1 . Avenue Liquors and Bar
2 . Belvedere Hotel
3 . Latrobe Building
4 . Washington Monument
5 . Saint Vincent de Paul
6 . Phoenix Shot Tower
7 . Gardel's
8 . USS Constellation
9 . National Aquarium
10. Bertha's
11. Cat's Eye
12. Chubbie's
13. Patterson Theater
14. Matthew's Pizzeria
15. O'Donnell Square